COCKTAILS
a complete guide

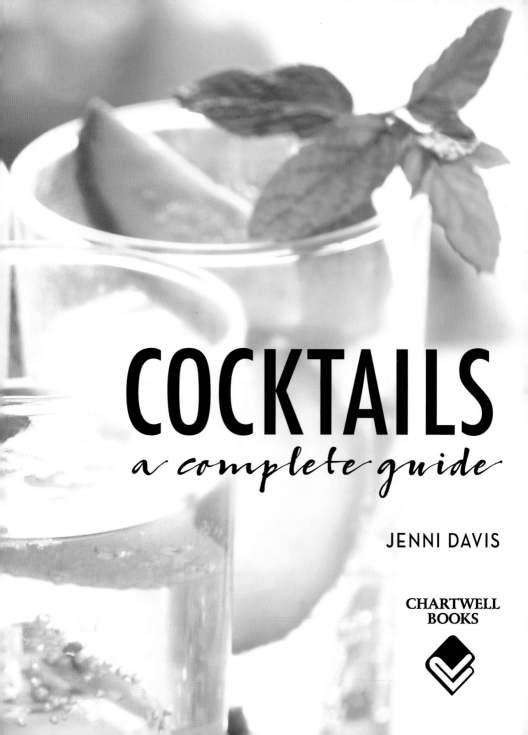

COCKTAILS
a complete guide

JENNI DAVIS

CHARTWELL
BOOKS

Inspiring | Educating | Creating | Entertaining

Brimming with creative inspiration, how-to projects, and useful information to enrich your everyday life, Quarto Knows is a favorite destination for those pursuing their interests and passions. Visit our site and dig deeper with our books into your area of interest: Quarto Creates, Quarto Cooks, Quarto Homes, Quarto Lives, Quarto Drives, Quarto Explores, Quarto Gifts, or Quarto Kids.

This edition published in 2020 by Chartwell Books,
an imprint of The Quarto Group,
142 West 36th Street, 4th Floor, New York,
NY 10018, USA
T (212) 779-4972 F (212) 779-6058
www.QuartoKnows.com

Chartwell titles are also available at discount for retail, wholesale, promotional, and bulk purchase. For details, contact the Special Sales Manager by email at specialsales@quarto.com or by mail at The Quarto Group, Attn: Special Sales Manager, 100 Cummings Center Suite 265D, Beverly, MA 01915 USA.

QUAR CDI

Conceived, edited, and designed by
Quarto Publishing,
an imprint of The Quarto Grouo
The Old Brewery
6 Blundell Street
London N7 9BH

Picture researchers: Sarah Bell and Jenni Davis
Designer: Austin Taylor
Project managers: Jane Moseley and Jackie Strachan
Art director: Caroline Guest
Creative director: Moira Clinch
Publisher: Samantha Warrington

10 9 8 7 6 5 4 3 2 1

ISBN-13: 978-0-7858-3886-9

Printed in Singapore COS062020

Contents

Foreword

The art of distilling spirits was probably discovered in ancient Mesopotamia—modern-day Iraq—more than four thousand years ago. We should raise our glasses to some unknown hedonist, for without that happy invention the cocktail would never have lifted *our* spirits.

The common use of the term "cocktail" dates back to the early 1800s, although its origins are very much in dispute. There are at least 15 rational explanations as to how the term came about, or even where it first came about. *That* topic of discussion is best left for historians to pore over.

The real newsflash today is that the world is experiencing a dramatic rise in popularity of these mixed marvels, even if the cocktail culture now marches to a different beat. The appeal is scarcely surprising, when you consider the long and colorful history of the cocktail—shaken or stirred. So much more than a mere drink, the cocktail survived—or sustained—the Prohibition years to become the enduring symbol of elegance, synonymous with the legends of Hollywood and with the songs, the music of bars, lounges, and all the gin joints in all the towns in all the world...

Evolution, revolution, renaissance

So, which is it: Evolution, revolution, or renaissance? A bit of all three, no doubt, since the number of acceptable ingredients in a cocktail has expanded exponentially over the past ten years. There are more syrups, liqueurs, purées, flavorings, rimming spices, herbs, extracts, granulated peppers, and even fresh vegetation, all expanding the creator's palette as well as the recipient's palate. Still, it's not as if this direction in creation is something completely new. Or is it?

The cocktail was originally defined as a four-part concoction: distilled spirits, water, sugar, and bitters. That's it. That's what a cocktail was "in the good ol' days." The variety in flavor and aroma came from how much of each ingredient was used, and in what fashion. Was the drink stirred or shaken? How much sugar? What style of whiskey?

But in reality today's cocktails are better than they have ever been thanks to a greater understanding and appreciation of how different ingredients interact in the blend (or stay solo as layers), the use of only fresh ingredients, the skill of the mixer, and the quality of the components. Experimentation in cocktail preparation is a difficult temptation to avoid because using new

combinations of ingredients—even entirely new ingredients—is really fun.
When you earn the satisfaction of knowing you did something for the first
time, and others approve, that is quite a sense of accomplishment.

Yet every lover of cocktails and every professional mixologist must
eventually hark back to the Classics, those great drinks invented by previous
innovators whose creations have stood not only the test of time, but also the
test of enjoyment. For what is the cocktail if not an expression of elegance,
glamor, sparkle, and, above all, pleasure?

Looking ahead

Which brings us to *Cocktails: A Complete Guide*. Author Jenni Davis has
provided the 150 best cocktails of all time. Here are the essentials for anyone
who enjoys making cocktails, or enjoys drinking them. Or both, as it no doubt
is in most cases.

What is important to appreciate is that in order to create new dimensions,
you have to be well versed in the Classics. Your ultimate goal makes no
difference: First you learn from those who preceded you, then you build toward
where you want to go. That is simply the way with the human condition.

This volume, as exciting in its presentation as in its content, provides you
with an easy-to-follow route map of know-how. Once you have mastered the
Classics, then your personal enhancements take on new meanings, and new
pleasures result. Throughout there are margin-note suggestions, guiding you
to other recipes that are likely to please your palate. These helpful next-steps
expand your knowledge of cocktails, while at the same time taking particular
note of what you already know and enjoy. You get the lowdown on muddling,
shaking, choice of glass, and some neat ideas and inspiration for making your
drink look as good as it tastes.

We guarantee you will delight in this celebratory drinks guidebook. It's a
fabulous way to open new avenues for entertaining and being entertained.

Santé! Cin! Cin! Sláinte! Na zdraví! Salut! Prost! Skål! L' Chaim!
Kanpai! Zdorovye! Cheers!

Brenda Maitland and Tim McNally
FOUNDING MEMBERS OF THE BOARD OF THE MUSEUM OF THE AMERICAN COCKTAIL

Introduction

Welcome to the wonderful world of cocktails! And what a fun world it is—you'll find all the familiar basics (you know the ones—gin, vodka, whiskey, brandy, etc) transformed by a few magical ingredients into aperitifs to jump-start your appetite, after-dinner drinks to soothe your digestion, long, cool drinks for long, hot evenings, fresh and fruity drinks for lazy afternoons, and as for the final section—let's party!

A drink is a drink is a drink, but a cocktail is a thing of beauty. Enjoy every aspect of it, from choosing which cocktail to make to selecting the glass to serve it in, from the ritual of mixing the cocktail to the moment that you decant it into the glass. Take time to appreciate the color, the garnish, the frost on the glass; now close your eyes and take in the aroma, letting it heighten your senses; then take that first sip and—mmmm, let yourself drift away on the *taste...*

You and your cocktail can enjoy a beautiful experience in private, or you can get together and share your moment with friends. Cocktails are great for breaking the ice at a social gathering—because if all else fails, you can always make the cocktail the topic of conversation!

I very much hope that you'll enjoy this guide to the glorious art of cocktail making.

Jenni Davis

On a serious note

Throughout the book, I often make light of the intoxicating effects of cocktails, but please remember that, with the exception of a handful of "mocktails," they're all alcoholic, some extremely so. Obviously if you're making a cocktail for yourself you'll be aware of what goes into it and restrict your post-cocktail activities accordingly; however, if you're serving cocktails to guests, please make sure that they too are aware of what they're drinking.

Note also that cocktails including raw egg whites (or whole eggs, in the case of Eggnog) should be avoided by anyone with compromised health.

About this book

If you're a novice cocktail maker, the first thing to do is to read the Bar Code, pages 10–27. This tells you about the accouterments of cocktail making—the glasses, bar equipment, ingredients, and garnishes. And, most importantly, it tells you HOW—how to shake, how to stir, and how to layer. This information will enable you to venture with confidence toward the next step—making a cocktail.

When it comes to choosing a cocktail, you have a number of options.

1 Close the book, close your eyes, open the book at random, open your eyes, and whichever cocktail catches your eye is the one you'll make (sometimes there'll only be one, so you'll have no choice!).

2 If you'd like the process to be a little less adventurous, use the Cocktail Selector on pages 20–23. This lists all the cocktails in the book and also lists the alcoholic ingredients. An orange dot indicates which ingredients are in each cocktail, so that you can select cocktails containing your favorite spirit or liqueur. If there's no orange dot against a cocktail, it means that the recipe is a "mocktail"—no alcohol in there!

3 On each recipe page, "Like this? Try this" guides you to a cocktail that has an ingredient in common with the one you've made, so you can enjoy it in a different guise.

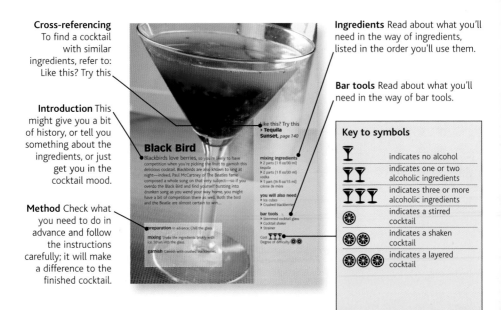

Cross-referencing To find a cocktail with similar ingredients, refer to: Like this? Try this

Introduction This might give you a bit of history, or tell you something about the ingredients, or just get you in the cocktail mood.

Method Check what you need to do in advance and follow the instructions carefully; it will make a difference to the finished cocktail.

Ingredients Read about what you'll need in the way of ingredients, listed in the order you'll use them.

Bar tools Read about what you'll need in the way of bar tools.

Black Bird

Blackbirds love berries, so you're likely to have competition when you're picking the fruit to garnish this delicious cocktail. Blackbirds are also known to sing at night—indeed, Paul McCartney of The Beatles fame composed a whole song on that very subject—so if you overdo the Black Bird and find yourself bursting into drunken song as you wend your way home, you might have a bit of competition there as well. Both the bird and the Beatle are almost certain to win.

preparation In advance. Chill the glass.

mixing Shake the ingredients briskly with ice. Strain into the glass.

garnish Garnish with crushed blackberries.

Like this? Try this
▸ **Tequila Sunset**, page 140

mixing ingredients
▸ 2 parts (1 fl oz/30 ml) tequila
▸ 2 parts (1 fl oz/30 ml) vodka
▸ 1 part (½ fl oz/15 ml) crème de mûre

you will also need
▸ Ice cubes
▸ Crushed blackberries

bar tools
▸ Stemmed cocktail glass
▸ Cocktail shaker
▸ Strainer

Cost ΥΥΥ
Degree of difficulty

Key to symbols	
Υ	indicates no alcohol
ΥΥ	indicates one or two alcoholic ingredients
ΥΥΥ	indicates three or more alcoholic ingredients
✹	indicates a stirred cocktail
✹✹	indicates a shaken cocktail
✹✹✹	indicates a layered cocktail

Bar Code

1

| Martini glass | Margarita glass | Lowball glass | Highball glass |

Equipment

Cocktail making is a wonderful ritual and, like the Japanese tea ceremony, benefits from the appropriate equipment.

The glass

The glass in which you serve your drink plays a huge part in the magical cocktail experience, so let's give the matter the careful consideration it deserves.

▶ **Martinis** just adore showing off in the classic cocktail glass, its generous proportions the perfect shape to embrace your favorite martini and its garnish.

▶ **Margaritas** are happiest in an authentic margarita glass, which opens out wide at the top to give you a really generous rim for the traditional garnish of salt.

▶ **The more rugged cocktails,** served over ice, like to assert themselves in a short tumbler known as a lowball glass (or sometimes called a rocks glass or an Old Fashioned glass).

▶ **Simple long cocktails** sit comfortably in a taller tumbler known as a highball glass. This can be a no-nonsense straight-up-and-down glass or a pretty one.

▶ **"Look-at-me"** long cocktails want to be admired in a curvy stemmed glass, such as a hurricane or tall tulip glass.

▶ **Shots** have special little glasses to accommodate them. Their small stature belies the strength of their contents, which tends to be way out of proportion.

▶ **Champagne cocktails** expect to be served in a glass that reflects their luxurious, even regal nature. A champagne flute is really the only option here.

▶ **Warm or hot cocktails** need a glass with a handle so that you can relish them without burning your fingers.

Tulip glass *Shot glass* *Champagne flute* *Cobbler shaker*

The cocktail shaker

The shaker is the jewel in the crown of cocktail equipment. It's worth investing in one for the pleasure it brings to the ritual of cocktail making.

Thousands of years ago, the South Americans discovered that a hollowed-out gourd, reunited with its lid, made a very useful container for shaking things up— and the rest, as they say, is history. The modern shaker began to emerge in the mid 19th-century, after an innkeeper observed that if you put two tumblers together, open end to open end, and one tumbler is slightly smaller than the other, it creates a very effective seal and you

can not only shake up your ingredients but also make something of a show of doing it. Within no time at all, commercial shakers were being produced.

There are three types of shaker, but the two most popular are:

▶ **The Cobbler Shaker** This one's an absolute beauty. It's elegantly shaped and comes with a built-in strainer. If you get one with a cap that's marked to serve as a measure, you won't need to use a separate jigger.

▶ **The Boston Shaker** This is more rudimentary in design but that 19th-century innkeeper would be proud to see that it's very like his accidental discovery. It consists of a metal bottom and a mixing glass and it has the advantage that the mixing glass can be used for mixing (obviously!), stirring, or muddling, with or without shaking afterwards. You need a separate strainer for this one.

The third type, the French Shaker, is a cross between the two—curvy, but in two sections, and it needs a separate strainer.

Plain is beautiful

Some glasses, especially martini and shot glasses, are available covered with gimmicky decoration. They can be fun— but when it comes to cocktails, they're all wrong. The cocktail itself is the star, and the glass can only hope for the accolade of Best Supporting Role. So your glass can be a beautiful shape, but apart from that—keep it simple.

Measure

Bartenders and cocktail aficionados use a cute little double-ended tool for measuring the ingredients, called a jigger. Although a jigger doesn't come in a standard size, typically (and most usefully) it has a jigger-sized cone at one end—that's 1.5 fl oz (45 ml)—and a pony-sized cone at the other. A pony, or shot, is 1 fl oz (30 ml). So that you don't end up in a confusion of jiggers and ponies when making the cocktails in this book, we've given the measurements in "parts," which, if you're using a jigger, works out like this:

> ▶ 1 part = ½ pony (½ fl oz/15 ml)
> ▶ 2 parts = 1 pony (1 fl oz/30 ml)
> ▶ 3 parts = 1 jigger (1½ fl oz/45 ml)
> ▶ 4 parts = 2 ponies (2 fl oz/60 ml)
> ▶ 5 parts = 1 jigger + 1 pony or 2½ ponies (2½ fl oz/75 ml)
> ▶ 6 parts = 2 jiggers or 3 ponies (3 fl oz/90 ml)
> ▶ 8 parts = 4 ponies (4 fl oz/120 ml)

Keep it in proportion
Whatever method you use to measure your ingredients, the important thing is to keep to the proportions specified in the recipe, or your cocktail simply won't be authentic. Only an experienced bartender can mix a cocktail by eye and get it perfect every time!

If you don't have a jigger, you can of course use anything you have to hand that will measure a volume roughly equivalent to a "part." An alternative is to use measuring spouts on your bottles. These have little ball bearings that let the spout release only a certain amount of liquid—one size releases ¼ fl oz/7.5 ml, another 1½ fl oz/45 ml.

Muddler

Muddling is a wonderful practice that involves placing, for example, mint and sugar in a glass and giving it a good—muddle! The muddler (below) is simply a wooden cylinder with a gently rounded end, sometimes grooved, and the idea is to crush your muddling ingredients to release the aroma, or juice, or whatever other treasures they contain. You can use a wooden spoon instead, but somehow there's not the same magic.

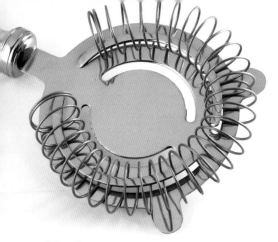

Strainer

The strainer (above) is used with a Boston shaker or a mixing glass and it's essential to have one to filter out stray bits of ice, citrus pulp, and anything else that would spoil the harmony of your cocktail. You'll need one of these whenever the recipe method says: "Strain into the cocktail glass."

Bar spoon

A proper bar spoon will make you feel like a real bartender—and it's a lovely thing to own, anyway. It has a very long handle, often elegantly turned, and a disc at one end to add vigor to your stirring. You also use a bar spoon for making layered shots.

Bar knife

This has a serrated edge for slicing citrus fruits, a split point for spearing citrus wedges or slices, and usually an integral bottle cap opener also. It's not essential as no doubt you'll have a sharp kitchen knife that will do the job, but they're often included in a cocktail set.

Borrowed from the kitchen...

▸ **Blender** This is really useful for mixing up frozen margaritas, daiquiris etc. You just throw in all the ingredients with a lot of crushed ice, and your cocktail is ready in seconds. A food processor does the same job but it's slightly less convenient to decant from.

▸ **Juice extractor** If you have one of these, you'll be able to make the most fantastic fruity cocktails. A piña colada with pineapple juice from a carton is okay, but made with freshly squeezed juice it's sensational.

▸ **Citrus press** This doesn't need to be at all sophisticated—a wooden reamer or porcelain citrus juicer costs next to nothing and will do the job perfectly well.

▸ **Citrus channeler** Use this handy little tool to make long strips of zest (practice makes perfect!), which you can curl into a twist or tie into a knot.

▸ **Potato peeler** A swivel potato peeler is great for making long strands of citrus or apple peel with artistically ragged edges, to twist as a garnish.

"Top-shelf" liquor

In bartending language, top-shelf liquor is the very best premium brand, which is only used if you specify it. If you ask for a cocktail but don't mention a particular name, it'll be made with the lesser—but nonetheless good—brand that's kept on the "speed rack," the collection of liquors, mixers, etc arranged at easily accessible counter-height.

Setting up a home bar

Never does the saying "You get what you pay for" carry more truth than when you're referring to cocktail ingredients.

A cocktail is a treat, an indulgence, an absolute luxury—but it will only be as good as the ingredients you use. It's a temptation, of course, to reason that a bottle of gin that could double up as paint-stripper will do perfectly well because it'll be mixed with other things, but a cocktail is a delicate balance of flavors designed to complement each other perfectly, and the last thing you want is to detect an undertone of something slightly unpleasant.

Personal taste differs, of course, and in most cases there's no problem at all with using your preferred brand—just as long as that brand happens to be a really good one!

Stocking up

To help you choose what to stock up on, take a look at the Cocktail Selector on pages 20–23, which names the liquors (or spirits, if your prefer) and liqueurs used in the main recipes in this book. Even without the variations it's a long list, so before you break open your coin bank and head for the store, decide what ingredient you'd most like to include. If your top tipple is vodka, for example, you can quickly find all the cocktails containing vodka, see what other ingredients are needed, and start with the one that appeals to you most. Then you can try a different cocktail containing one of the other ingredients, and so on!

Surf the net

If you can't find an ingredient in your supermarket or liquor store, check out the internet—even the more obscure ingredients are available by mail order.

Variations on a theme

You might think that rum is rum and schnapps is schnapps and—perish the thought!—whiskey is whiskey, but no. Virtually everything has a variation of some sort (and whiskey, of course, even has a variant spelling—if it's Scotch or Canadian, it's whisky). With a few exceptions, the type or flavor listed in the recipe is the one to use, because it's the one that gives that particular cocktail its distinctive character.

When it comes to brand names, you have a little more choice—but make sure you read the cautionary note about quality, above! There are several brands available of virtually everything, even the more unusual things such as the rather bizarre flavors of vodka and schnapps— whoever dreamed up chocolate vodka or butterscotch schnapps?

Liqueurs

Liqueurs are a wonderful invention— in many recipes, they build on the basic liquor and transform it into something extraordinary. Some liqueurs, such as Chartreuse and Bénédictine, are based on recipes that have been in existence for several hundred years, their ingredients remaining a closely guarded secret, while others are very definitely a modern innovation. Even tequila, a fairly macho liquor, has got in touch with its feminine side and forms the base for a strawberry cream liqueur. Chocoholics can revel in white or dark chocolate liqueurs, caffeine addicts can get their after-dinner coffee and liqueur in one hit, and the health-conscious can choose from a whole range of fruit liqueurs and thereby pretend to be addressing their recommended daily intake.

A word about citrus juice

Freshly made juice is wonderful and will lift a fruity cocktail to giddy heights, but most fruits are difficult to juice without an electric juice extractor. If you don't have one of these, a good-quality brand in a carton or bottle is a good compromise. However, citrus fruits are really easy to juice with a simple reamer or even your hands, so there's *absolutely no excuse* to use anything but freshly squeezed citrus juices in your cocktails. Nothing else will do!

Sugar syrup

Several recipes include a measure of simple sugar syrup. You can buy this, but it's really easy to make yourself. Place 1 part sugar with 1 part water in a small saucepan, bring to a boil, then simmer until the sugar is dissolved. Let cool completely, then store in a glass jar with a lid in the refrigerator for up to a month.

Sweet and sour mix

To make your own sweet and sour mix, first make a sugar syrup as above, but in the proportions 3 parts sugar to 2 parts water. Now mix 1 part of the sugar syrup

Rainbow colors

Well, most of them, at least. You can have really good fun making colorful cocktails—Midori® will give you a bright green drink, while grenadine adds a splash of bright red. But the most dramatic color—probably because it's so far removed from anything you would expect to see—is the electric blue created by blue curaçao. The curaçao itself is wonderfully natural, the color very definitely NOT. It's fun, fabulous, and well worth stocking in your bar cabinet.

with 1 part freshly squeezed lemon juice and it's done. Store as for simple syrup.

Bitters

Bitters either stimulate the appetite or settle the stomach, so they are an excellent addition to an aperitif or digestif cocktail. You'll find two types of bitters mentioned in this book—Angostura and orange. Angostura aromatic bitters have a high alcohol content (but you only ever use a dash or two), and are flavored with gentian. They come in a fairly small bottle with a distinctive oversized label, which looks like a packaging hand-me-down. Orange bitters, made with the peel of Seville oranges, are traditionally used in some of the classic cocktails and went out of vogue for a while—but now they're back!

Cordially yours

Grenadine is a very sweet red cordial, or syrup, used in lots of cocktail recipes. Traditionally it's made from pomegranate juice, but many commercial brands have completely lost sight of this and the ingredients are all artificial. Seek out a good brand, or make your own—mix pomegranate juice with an equal amount of sugar, bring to a boil, then simmer until syrupy. Store as for simple syrup (above).

Bottled lime juice (known as lime cordial in the UK) is used in a Gimlet and there's only one brand to use—Rose's®. Anything else and it's not a Gimlet!

The big chill

Cocktails are very cool indeed—and are at their best served that way! Make sure you're always prepared for when the cocktail mood is upon you.

Ice

The ice is such an important part of cocktail making that it almost deserves a book in its own right. Okay, that's a bit of an exaggeration, but at least it makes the point! If you're using a shaker, the ice goes in the shaker. If you're mixing in a glass, the ice goes in the glass. Sometimes you shake the cocktail with ice and then decant it over ice. Sometimes you blend the ingredients with ice. There are very few recipes in this book that don't involve—ICE!

Chilling the ingredients

Storing your cocktail ingredients in the refrigerator is a really good habit to get into. Yes, the ingredients are going to be getting up close and personal with quite a lot of ice, but the idea of that is to chill the ingredients even more, not to thaw the ice and dilute the cocktail. So even if you're going to make a cocktail in a shaker, keep those liquors and liqueurs chilled. It's even more important when you're making a cocktail with fizz, such as a champagne cocktail, because the fizz is added separately, and it's absolutely essential for a layered cocktail, when no ice is used at all.

Chilling the glass

An organized person will put their cocktail glass in the refrigerator well ahead of time and it will be deliciously chilled. If you don't fit that description (and how many of us do?), the alternative is to fill the glass with ice (which of course you *will* have made in advance) when you start assembling the cocktail, then simply discard the ice before you pour in your drink.

Four steps to perfect ice cubes

1 Use fresh, clean, bottled or filtered water to make ice—only use unfiltered tap water if it comes straight from the spring.

2 Make your ice cubes in special trays or bags. Flexible trays are perfect—it's easy to turn out the ice, and they come in some crazy novelty shapes.

3 Position open trays well away from any foods that might taint the ice. Fishy shapes are one thing, a fishy flavor is quite another.

4 Keep several trays in the freezer (you'll need plenty of ice) and remember to rotate them so that your ice is always fresh.

Cocktail selector

liquors

Category	Cocktail	gin	Pimms No 1®	vodka	vodka (lemon)	vodka (vanilla)	vodka (raspberry)	vermouth (dry)	vermouth (sweet)	tequila	schnapps (peach)	schnapps (butterscotch)	schnapps (apple)	schnapps (strawberry)	schnapps (tangerine)	whiskey (rye)	whiskey (bourbon)	whiskey (Irish)	whisky (Scotch)	whisky (Canadian)	brandy	brandy (apricot)	brandy (cherry)	brandy (kirsch)	rum (white)	rum (gold)	rum (dark)	rum (spiced)	rum (coconut)	absinthe	sambuca (red)	Campari®	cachaça	port
Aperitifs	Bacardi Cocktail																								●									
	Black Bird			●						●																								
	*Dry Martini	●						●																										
	Lemon Twist Martini			●				●																										
	Manhattan								●							●	●																	
	Ink Martini				●						●																							
	*Betty Blue			●				●		●																								
	*Eden	●																														●		
	Margarita									●																								
	Blue Margarita									●																								
	Bronx	●						●	●																									
	Old-fashioned															●																		
	Cowboy Hoof	●																																
	Gimlet	●																																
	Daiquiri																								●									
	*White Lady	●																																
	Kyoto	●						●																										
	*Whiskey Sour																●																	
	Blue Shark			●						●																								
	Bramble	●																																
After-dinner Drinks	Irish Coffee																	●																
	Captain's Coffee																											●						
	Carrot Cake Shot											●																						
	Brandy Alexander																				●													
	*Brandy-Apricot Cocktail																				●													
	Sombrero																																	
	Barbara			●																														
	Grasshopper																																	
	Cockroach																																	
	*B-52																																	
	*White Russian			●																														
	American Beauty							●													●													●
	*Chocolatini					●																												
	Heather's Pleasure																																	
	White Heather																		●															
	Green Dragon			●																														
	Tricolor																														●			
	Creamsicle					●																												
	*Sidecar																				●													
	Fireball Shot																													●	●			
Long and Cool	*Mai Tai																								●									
	Blue Hawaii			●																					●									
	Blue Lagoon			●																														
	New York																			●														
	Island Breeze																								●									
	*Gin Rickey	●																																
	Long Island Iced Tea	●		●						●															●									
	*Singapore Sling	●																					●											
	*Tom Collins	●																																
	Caipirinha																																●	

* indicates recipe has variations   ● main ingredient   ● alternative ingredient

	liqueurs																																				fizz	
	Cointreau®	Grand Marnier®	Chartreuse®	Bénédictine®	Tuaca®	Galliano®	Kahlúa®	Amarula®	Passoa®	Chambord®	curaçao (blue)	curaçao (orange)	triple sec	orange liqueur	strawberry liqueur	raspberry liqueur	peach liqueur	apricot liqueur	melon liqueur	banana liqueur	vanilla liqueur	crème de noyaux	crème de banane	crème de cassis	crème de mûre	crème de cacao (white)	crème de cacao (dark)	crème de menthe (green)	crème de menthe (white)	lemon cream	coffee liqueur	chocolate liqueur	Irish Cream liqueur	whiskey liqueur	heather cream		champagne	prosecco
																								●													
										●																											
										●																											
										●																											
	●																																					
																		●																				
										●																											
									●															●													
																														●							
																																●					
																									●	●											
																	●																				
						●																															
																									●												
																									●		●										
																														●			●				
		●						●																						●		●					
																														●							
																													●								
																															●						
																															●			●			
																						●			●												
			●																																			
																														●								
					●							●																									
													●																								
											●																										
										●																											
										●																											
												●																									
	●			●																																		

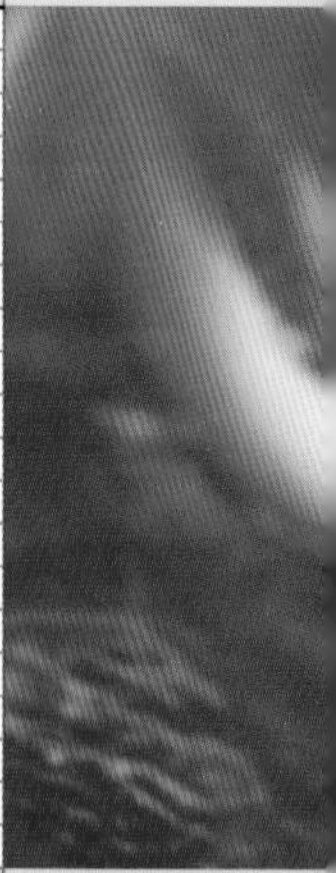

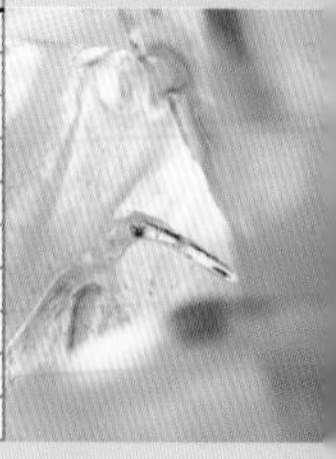

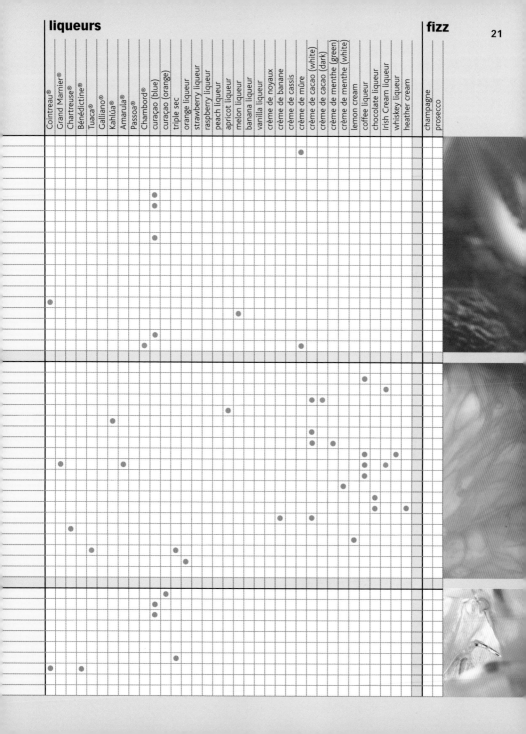

Cocktail selector

liquors

Cocktail	gin	Pimms No 1®	vodka	vodka (lemon)	vodka (vanilla)	vodka (raspberry)	vermouth (dry)	vermouth (sweet)	tequila	schnapps (peach)	schnapps (butterscotch)	schnapps (apple)	schnapps (strawberry)	schnapps (tangerine)	whiskey (rye)	whiskey (bourbon)	whiskey (Irish)	whisky (Scotch)	whisky (Canadian)	brandy	brandy (apricot)	brandy (cherry)	brandy (kirsch)	rum (white)	rum (gold)	rum (dark)	rum (spiced)	rum (coconut)	absinthe	sambuca (red)	Campari®	cachaça	port
Long and Cool																																	
Hurricane																								●	●								
*Americano								●																							●		
Mojito																								●									
Cuba Libre																								●	●								
Harvey Wallbanger			●																														
Mint Julep																●																	
Babar			●																														
Woo-Woo			●							●																							
Chili Queen																																	
Runner's Mark																																	
Fresh and Fruity																																	
Pimm's®		●																															
*Banana Punch			●																		●												
Appletini			●									●																					
Frozen Margaritas									●																								
Pomegranate Mojito																								●									
Jamaican Sunset																										●	●						
Operation Recoverer				●										●																			
Lemonade																																	
Carambola Cocktail			●																			●											
Tropical Martini	●																																
*Tequila Sunrise									●																								
Raspberry Cosmo						●																											
Sea Breeze			●																														
*Piña Colada																								●									
Screwdriver			●																														
Alien Sky																					●		●	●									
Russian Spring			●																														
*Bloody Mary			●																														
French Martini			●																														
*Gin Fizz	●																																
Let's Party																																	
Buck's Fizz																																	
Grass Skirt	●																																
Strawberry Daiquiri													●											●									
*Red Cloud	●																				●												
Brandy Zoom																				●													
Rose							●															●	●										
*Bellini																																	
*Kir Royal																																	
Kamikaze			●																														
*Cosmopolitan				●																													
Yum-Yum																								●				●					
Mediterranean Martini	●					●																											
Cranberry Champagne Cocktail																																	
The Kiss			●																														
Pink Elephant			●																														
Flirtini			●																														
Zombie																					●			●		●							
Electric Lemonade				●																													
*Fireworks	●												●																				
Eggnog																				●							●						

* indicates recipe has variations ● main ingredient ● alternative ingredient

liqueurs

fizz

Cointreau®	Grand Marnier®	Chartreuse®	Bénédictine®	Tuaca®	Galliano®	Kahlúa®	Amarula®	Passoa®	Chambord®	curaçao (blue)	curaçao (orange)	triple sec	orange liqueur	strawberry liqueur	raspberry liqueur	peach liqueur	apricot liqueur	melon liqueur	banana liqueur	vanilla liqueur	crème de noyaux	crème de banane	crème de cassis	crème de mûre	crème de cacao (white)	crème de cacao (dark)	crème de menthe (green)	crème de menthe (white)	lemon cream liqueur	coffee liqueur	chocolate liqueur	Irish Cream liqueur	whiskey liqueur	heather cream	champagne	prosecco
					●																															
								●																												
																			●																	
																		●																		
												●																								
												●																								
									●																											
																											●								●	
								●						●																					
																																			●	
												●																								
																																				●
																							●												●	
										●																										
																●																				
										●																										
													●																						●	
														●																						
																				●	●															
												●																							●	
										●																										
																																			●	

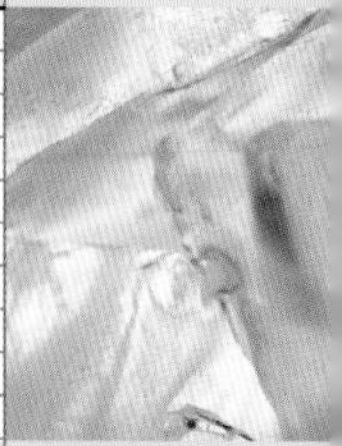

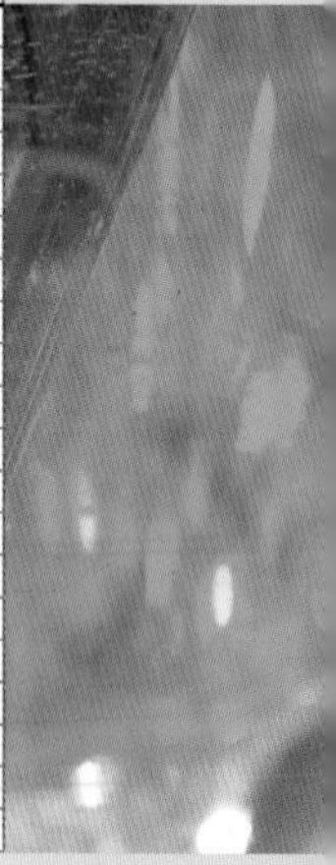

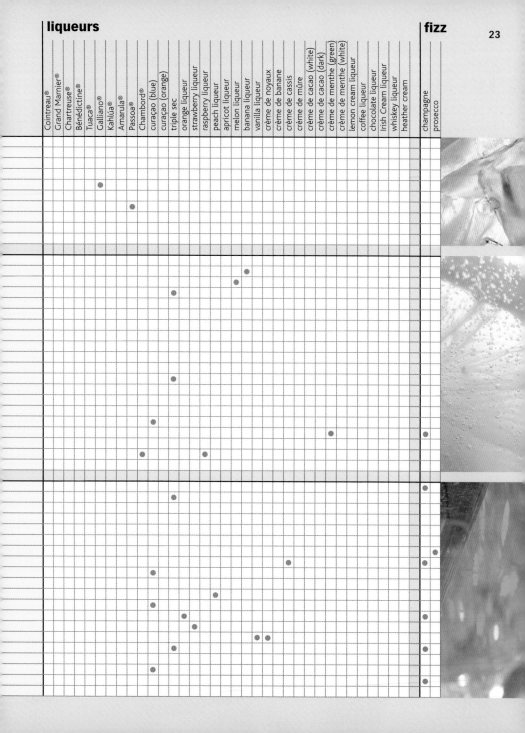

Techniques

Cocktails are usually made by one of three methods—they are shaken, stirred, or layered. Shaking is easy and fun; stirring is easy and there's not much fun involved, but it gets the job done; layering is a real skill, but once you've mastered it you'll feel very smug indeed. Here's how it's all done.

Shake it all about

Cocktail making is a great opportunity for showmanship, and even the untrained home bartender can make a big deal of it when it comes to mixing in a shaker. You fill the shaker with ice; you add the ingredients; you shake, shake, shake; you decant a beautiful, delicious cocktail into the glass you chilled earlier; then mmmm, that first sip! This is how to make a perfect cocktail in a shaker, step by step:

1 If the recipe includes freshly squeezed citrus juice, freshly squeeze it now. If the recipe includes any other fresh juice and you have a juice extractor, now is the time to use it.

2 Assemble all the ingredients.

3 Fill the shaker with ice, almost to the top.

4 Measure out the ingredients and add them to the shaker.

5 Now the fun bit. Put the cap on the shaker (getting covered in ice and cocktail ingredients is not part of the fun)

and shake it like your life depends on it. In the method, we call it shaking briskly, but what we really mean is, hold the shaker at an angle and shake it up and down over your right shoulder, then over your left, then above your head—and remember to SMILE! Shake for about 20 seconds, or until the shaker frosts on the outside, and the chill begins to creep into your fingers... You can stop now!

6 Decant the cocktail into the glass— remember to use a strainer if your shaker doesn't have an integral one.

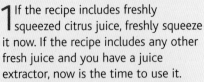

Flair bartending

This is the art of stylish cocktail bartending— juggling with daring, mixing with panache, shaking with attitude. John "JB" Bandy, winner of the first ever Flair Bartending World Championship, choreographed the 1988 movie *Cocktail* and trained Tom Cruise for his role as a bartender – but in spite of Cruise's undeniable skill, the movie won a Golden Raspberry award for Worst Picture.

Stir things up

Some cocktails don't need shaking—they simply need a bit of a stir with a bar spoon. You either do this in the glass in which you're going to serve the cocktail (add ice, add ingredients, stir, serve) or in a mixing glass (add ice, add ingredients, stir, strain into the serving glass, serve). In some cases, a little muddling goes on before the stirring, and this is best done in a mixing glass—use the glass from your Boston shaker, if you have one.

> **Tip**
> When making the cocktail recipes, always read the method before you start mixing in case one of the ingredients is added separately at the end. Be especially wary of grenadine—it's often used to create a lovely sunrise or sunset effect, and if you mix it with the other ingredients you'll just end up with an alarmingly red sky.

> **Shaken not stirred**
> A shaken cocktail will be cloudy at first because the ice in the shaker frosts the ingredients, whereas a stirred cocktail will be clear (unless, of course, it contains a cream liqueur).

Layering

The principle behind layering is incredibly simple—the higher the specific gravity of the liquid, the heavier it is, so by using ingredients with different specific gravities, you can create layers. A good example is grenadine, which has a high specific gravity—even if you add it to the glass last, it will sink gracefully to the bottom. That's the science lesson over! The next thing to remember is that there is no ice involved when making a layered cocktail, so you have to think ahead and chill the ingredients well in advance—and also the shot glass and a bar spoon. So, say you're making a three-layer shot. Always follow the order given in the method, and start by pouring the first ingredient into the glass. Now take the chilled bar spoon, hold it right over the glass, and very slowly pour the next ingredient over the spoon. It will settle on top of the first ingredient. Now repeat with the last ingredient, which will settle over the middle layer. Have faith—it really will!

Dressing up

This is the *really* good bit! Cocktails have big, bold personalities and many are positively flamboyant, so you can have lots of fun with garnishes.

Some classic cocktails have an equally classic garnish and to change this could give your cocktail a severe identity crisis. Most, though, are less sensitive, so you can be as creative as you like, adding anything from an elegant slice of lemon to an entire fruitbowl, along with a purely decorative flourish. And some cocktails, of course, need no garnish at all—they are so beautiful in their own right that to add a garnish would be almost tactless!

Tip
Cut fruity garnishes at the last minute so that they're fresh and glistening with mouth-watering juice—the dried-out, been-hanging-around-for-hours look is simply not as appealing.

Edible garnishes

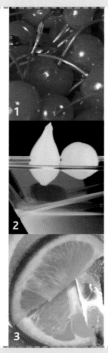

▶ **Maraschino cherries (1)**
Maraschino cherries are sweetened, preserved, and dyed an unnaturally bright red, but in spite of this they are very moreish, so they might not make it as far as your drink. They are a classic garnish for many cocktails.

▶ **Olives** A crisp green olive, with its slightly astringent flavor, is the perfect foil for a dry martini. This combo cannot fail to stimulate your appetite.

▶ **Marinated pearl onion (2)**
Strange though it might seem to garnish your cocktail with an onion, in certain cases it works! Thread two or three onto a cocktail pick.

▶ **Citrus fruits (3)** Whole slices, half slices, quarter slices, wedges, twists of zest—citrus fruit garnishes add a refreshing zing to a cocktail.

▶ **Fruits and veggies** For long cocktails, use anything that goes with the theme of the drink, with or without the citrus fruit—pineapple, banana, carambola, cucumber, even a stick of celery for a Bloody Mary.

▶ **Berries** *Fresh* raspberries, blackberries, and strawberries (frozen berries lose both their texture and their charm) make a great garnish for cocktails with the fruit in the name, such as Raspberry Cosmo, Bramble, and Strawberry Daiquiri. Cranberries

Decorative garnishes

▶ **Cocktail umbrellas (1)** The quintessential garnish for a sassy cocktail, these are brightly colored and come neatly rolled in boxes, ready for you to unfurl and pop in your drink. They go particularly well with cocktails with a sunshiny, tropical theme.

▶ **Cocktail picks (2)** These are for spearing your edible garnishes, and you can use an ordinary wooden toothpick for this purpose, but a decorative

cocktail pick is much more attractive (and far less likely to stab you).

▶ **Stirrer/swizzle sticks (3)** These are actually just sticks for stirring your cocktail, sometimes with a paddle at one end—all the better for stirring with. They come in some really fun, whacky designs and most cocktail bars will have their own customized stirrers (which of course they fully expect you to steal), so you can be forgiven if you find yourself turning into an avid collector of swizzles...

are best avoided as a garnish unless you have an unnatural liking for extremely sharp flavors.

▶ **Mint** An essential ingredient and garnish for some cocktails, and a pretty one for others. Grow fresh mint in a pot (it's rampant by nature) and, if the mood takes you, add a sprig to your cocktail whether it needs it or not!

▶ **Sprinkles (4)** Ground nutmeg or cinnamon, chocolate flakes, cocoa powder, and even cupcake sprinkles make lovely garnishes on a creamy cocktail.

▶ **Citrus zest shapes (5)** There are two ways to make these. Either use a channeling tool to cut a long strip of zest (it will

have some of the pith attached, which helps it keep its shape) and use it in its natural curl or tied into a knot, or use a potato peeler to peel a strip around the widest part of the fruit and form it into a twist (if it resists, shape it around the handle of a wooden spoon and freeze it quickly).

▶ **Citrus pinwheels (6)** Take a lemon, large lime, or orange and cut off the ends. Use a sharp knife to slice round the flesh, leaving the pith and zest intact. Remove the flesh with a spoon, leaving the shell. Cut through the shell, open it out, and roll it up tightly widthwise. Cut the rolled-up shell into slices and secure the pinwheels with cocktail picks.

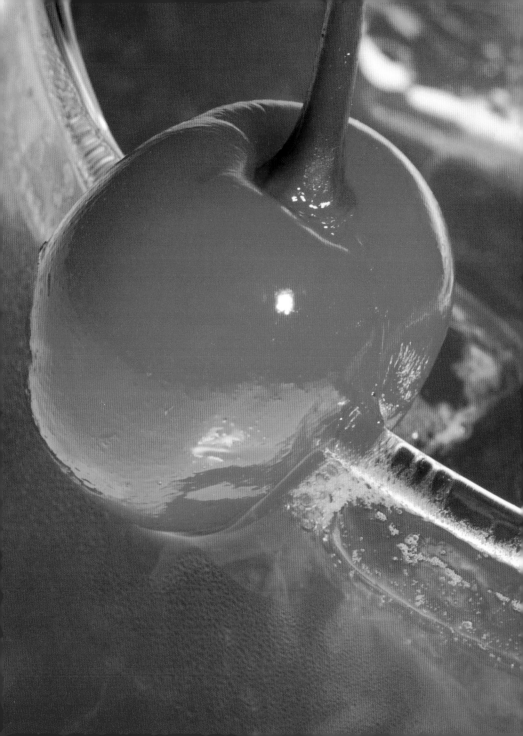

Aperitifs

2

Bacardi Cocktail

mixing ingredients
▶ 3 parts (1½ fl oz/45 ml) Bacardi® white rum
▶ 1½ parts (¾ fl oz/22.5 ml) freshly squeezed lime juice
▶ 1 teaspoon grenadine or sugar syrup

you will also need
▶ Ice cubes
▶ Maraschino cherry
▶ Lime wedge

bar tools
▶ Stemmed cocktail glass
▶ Cocktail shaker
▶ Strainer

Cost ¥¥
Degree of difficulty

Prohibition prompted some inventive departures from convention, such as using moonshine liquor and disguising the poor quality with added flavorings—replacing sugar syrup with grenadine, in the case of the Bacardi Cocktail. Bacardi were *not* impressed with this practice—a court ruling stated that "If it lacks Bacardi rum, no bartender's concoction can be called a Bacardi cocktail," while the 1951 *Bartender's Book* reported that "the Bacardi Company's efforts to educate the public away from [grenadine] have fallen upon deadened palates." So stick to Bacardi® rum, and add grenadine at your peril!

preparation In advance: Chill the glass.

mixing Shake the ingredients briskly with ice. Strain into the glass.

garnish Garnish with a maraschino cherry and a lime wedge.

Like this? Try this
▶ **Fireman's Sour,**
page 185

Black Bird

Blackbirds love berries, so you're likely to have competition when you're picking the fruit to garnish this delicious cocktail. Blackbirds are also known to sing at night—indeed, Paul McCartney of The Beatles fame composed a whole song on that very subject—so if you overdo the Black Bird and find yourself bursting into drunken song as you wend your way home, you might have a bit of competition there as well. Both the bird and the Beatle are almost certain to win...

preparation In advance: Chill the glass.

mixing Shake the ingredients briskly with ice. Strain into the glass.

garnish Garnish with crushed blackberries.

Like this? Try this
▸ **Tequila Sunset,** *page 140*

mixing ingredients
▸ 2 parts (1 fl oz/30 ml) tequila
▸ 2 parts (1 fl oz/30 ml) vodka
▸ 1 part (½ fl oz/15 ml) crème de mûre

you will also need
▸ Ice cubes
▸ Crushed blackberries

bar tools
▸ Stemmed cocktail glass
▸ Cocktail shaker
▸ Strainer

Cost ♈♈♈
Degree of difficulty

Dry Martini

A classic martini is a simple cocktail of gin and dry vermouth (wine infused with digestive herbs), served with an olive garnish. Nothing more, nothing less—although you might want to add a dash of orange bitters. It's stirred, not shaken—unless, like James Bond, you favor "shaken, not stirred." And if you *are* going to shake it, you must get the rhythm right—according to Nick Charles, the lead character in the 1934 comedy *The Thin Man*, you always shake a dry martini to waltz time. "Simple" can get very complicated...

mixing ingredients
▸ 3½ parts (1¾ fl oz/ 52.5 ml) gin
▸ 1 part (½ fl oz/15 ml) dry vermouth
▸ 1 dash orange bitters (optional)

you will also need
▸ Ice cubes
▸ Green olive

bar tools
▸ Stemmed cocktail glass
▸ Mixing glass
▸ Bar spoon
▸ Strainer

Cost ♈♈
Degree of difficulty 🍊

preparation In advance: Chill the cocktail glass.

mixing Stir the ingredients in the mixing glass with ice. Strain into the cocktail glass.

garnish Garnish with a green olive.

Like this? Try this
▸ **Bronx,** *page 45*

Gibson Martini

The Gibson in question is thought to be the American graphic artist Charles Dana Gibson who, when ordering a martini, scorned the traditional green olive garnish in favor of a silverskin onion. While you're feeling adventurous, try using Bombay Sapphire gin for added intrigue.

preparation In advance: Chill the cocktail glass.

mixing Pour the dry vermouth over ice in the mixing glass, stir well, then strain and discard the liquid. Add the gin to the glass and stir well. Strain into the cocktail glass.

garnish Garnish with a silverskin onion.

mixing ingredients
▶ ½ part (¼ fl oz/7.5 ml) dry vermouth
▶ 3 parts (1½ fl oz/45 ml) Bombay Sapphire® gin

you will also need
▶ Ice cubes
▶ Silverskin onion

bar tools
▶ Stemmed cocktail glass
▶ Mixing glass
▶ Bar spoon
▶ Strainer

Cost 🍸🍸
Degree of difficulty ⊛

Saketini

No, it's not authentic, but it's fun! Keep the gin but abandon the dry vermouth and instead use a little sake (Japanese rice wine). Garnish your saketini with slices of Japanese cucumber and serve with sushi. If, after a couple of glasses, you can say "sushi and saketini" instead of "sashay and suketini," treat yourself to another!

preparation In advance: Chill the glass.

mixing Shake the ingredients briskly with ice. Strain into the glass.

garnish Garnish with slices of Japanese cucumber.

mixing ingredients
▶ 5 parts (2½ fl oz/ 75 ml) gin
▶ ½ part (¼ fl oz/7.5 ml) dry sake

you will also need
▶ Ice cubes
▶ Japanese cucumber slices

bar tools
▶ Stemmed cocktail glass
▶ Cocktail shaker
▶ Strainer

Cost 🍸🍸
Degree of difficulty ⊛⊛

Lemon Twist Martini

Hate gin, love vodka? Then this is the martini of your dreams. You can keep it simple, using vodka, vermouth, and a lemon twist to garnish, or give it an extra citrus kick by using lemon-flavored vodka. For an intriguing variation that abandons convention completely, use lemon-flavored rum instead of vodka. Okay, so it's not strictly a martini—but who cares, it tastes good!

mixing ingredients
▸ 6 parts (3 fl oz/90 ml) vodka
▸ 2 parts (1 fl oz/30 ml) dry vermouth
OR
▸ 6 parts (3 fl oz/90 ml) lemon vodka or rum
▸ 1 part (½ fl oz/15 ml) dry vermouth

you will also need
▸ Ice cubes
▸ Twist of lemon zest

bar tools
▸ Stemmed cocktail glass
▸ Cocktail shaker
▸ Strainer

Cost ♟♟
Degree of difficulty

preparation In advance: Chill the glass.

mixing Shake the ingredients briskly with ice. Strain into the glass.

garnish Garnish with a twist of lemon.

Like this? Try this
▸ **Green Dragon,**
page 84

Like this? Try this
▶ **New York,**
page 98

Manhattan

No prizes for guessing what this one is named after! The original Manhattan cocktail dates back to the New York of the 1800s, when it was made with locally distilled rye whiskey rather than the more mellow bourbon made from corn, and was always stirred, not shaken. Today the Manhattan basks in the glory of descriptions such as "the king of cocktails" and "the drinking man's cocktail," and has played cameo roles in any number of movies and TV shows. Is yours a Manhattan?

preparation In advance: Chill the cocktail glass.

mixing Place ice cubes in the mixing glass. Add all the ingredients and stir well. Strain into the cocktail glass.

garnish Garnish with a maraschino cherry.

mixing ingredients

▶ 6 parts (3 fl oz/90 ml) rye whiskey or bourbon
▶ 3 parts (1½ fl oz/45 ml) sweet vermouth
▶ 1 or 2 drops Angostura® bitters

you will also need

▶ Ice cubes
▶ Maraschino cherry

bar tools

▶ Stemmed cocktail glass
▶ Mixing glass
▶ Bar spoon
▶ Strainer

Cost ΥΥ
Degree of difficulty

Ink Martini

Have you ever gone to the store with the intention of buying the really essential things in life—milk and a loaf of bread, perhaps—only to come back *without* the milk and bread, but with something completely pointless, such as a sachet of squid ink, which sounded fascinating but you'll never actually use? Well, in case you've done just that, here is a recipe for a squid ink martini. No? Okay, leave the squid ink to continue gathering dust and try this instead—it looks just like old-fashioned ink but it tastes delicious and there's nothing even remotely revolting in it, just an appetizing blend of fruit flavors.

mixing ingredients
▶ 2 parts (1 fl oz/30 ml) lemon vodka
▶ 1½ parts (¾ fl oz/22.5 ml) blue curaçao
▶ 1 part (½ fl oz/15 ml) peach schnapps
▶ 1 part (½ fl oz/15 ml) cranberry juice

you will also need
▶ Ice cubes
▶ Orange slice
▶ Decorative cocktail pick

bar tools
▶ Stemmed cocktail glass
▶ Cocktail shaker
▶ Strainer

Cost
Degree of difficulty ✦✦

preparation In advance: Chill the glass.

mixing Shake the ingredients briskly with ice. Strain into the glass.

garnish Garnish with an orange slice on a decorative cocktail pick.

Like this? Try this
▶ **Operation Recoverer,** *page 135*

Betty Blue

Betty is a name with some entertaining cocktail associations. The character Betty Flanigan in James Fenimore Cooper's *The Spy* (1821) was inspired by a tavern owner called Catherine Hustler—the lady who is said to have stirred a drink with a rooster's tail feather and thus invented the cocktail. Another Betty ran a famous bar in Detroit, and although Betty's Cocktail Lounge has now vanished, its memory survives in a rather cool T-shirt bearing an image of a scantily clad lady reclining in a giant cocktail glass...

mixing ingredients
▶ 3 parts (1½ fl oz/45 ml) vodka
▶ 1 part (½ fl oz/15 ml) peach schnapps
▶ 1 part (½ fl oz/15 ml) dry vermouth
▶ 3 drops blue curaçao

you will also need
▶ Ice cubes
▶ Maraschino cherry

bar tools
▶ Stemmed cocktail glass
▶ Cocktail shaker
▶ Strainer

Cost ♈♈♈
Degree of difficulty

preparation In advance: Chill the glass.

mixing Shake the ingredients briskly with ice. Strain into the glass.

garnish Garnish with a maraschino cherry.

Like this? Try this
▶ **Woo Woo,**
page 121

Wild Black Betty

This Betty simply must be a cowgirl in the Wild West, a gal with flashing dark eyes and flowing black hair, who rides like the wind and can drink any man under the table... Serve this cocktail in a shot glass and knock it back. Wild Black Betty would drink it that way.

preparation In advance: Chill the glass.

mixing Shake the ingredients briskly with ice. Strain into the glass.

mixing ingredients
▶ ½ tablespoon bourbon
▶ ½ tablespoon Tennessee whiskey
▶ ½ tablespoon peach liqueur
▶ ½ tablespoon grenadine
▶ ½ tablespoon lime juice

you will also need
▶ Ice cubes

bar tools
▶ Shot glass
▶ Cocktail shaker
▶ Strainer

Cost **YYY**
Degree of difficulty ◉◉

Betty Mac

John or Jane Doe is someone whose identity is unknown. "Mac" is a name traditionally used when informally addressing a man whose identity is unknown, so presumably a Betty Mac is the cocktail equivalent of a Jane Doe. Well, we might not know who she is, but she's a pretty good cocktail!

preparation In advance: Chill the glass.

mixing Pour the gin, sweet vermouth, and orange liqueur over ice in the glass. Add the grenadine and stir.

garnish Garnish with an orange slice.

mixing ingredients
▶ 2 parts (1 fl oz/30 ml) gin
▶ 1 part (½ fl oz/15 ml) sweet vermouth
▶ ½ tablespoon orange liqueur
▶ 1 dash grenadine

you will also need
▶ Ice cubes
▶ Orange slice

bar tools
▶ Lowball glass
▶ Bar spoon

Cost **YYY**
Degree of difficulty

Garden of Eden

You make one silly mistake, someone gets hold of the story, and people are still talking about it thousands of years later. Poor Adam and Eve—how were they to know, when they plucked the fruit from the Tree of the Knowledge of Good and Evil in the Garden of Eden, that it would turn into such a big deal? But some good will come of everything, such as this cocktail.

mixing ingredients
▶ 2 parts (1 fl oz/30 ml) Southern Comfort®
▶ 3 parts (1½ fl oz/45 ml) melon liqueur
▶ ½ part (¼ fl oz/7.5 ml) freshly squeezed lime juice

you will also need
▶ Ice cubes

bar tools
▶ Stemmed cocktail glass
▶ Cocktail shaker
▶ Strainer

Cost ♈♈
Degree of difficulty 🍊🍊

preparation In advance: Chill the glass.

mixing Shake the ingredients briskly with ice. Strain into the glass.

Dusk in Eden

Just what *was* the fruit that Eve picked from the tree in the Garden of Eden, urged on by that unscrupulous serpent? Scholars are still trying to solve the puzzle. Traditionally it's portrayed as an apple, but it could also have been a quince, a peach, an apricot, a pomegranate—hmm, let's go with that...

mixing ingredients
▶ 1 tablespoon pomegranate seeds
▶ ½ teaspoon sugar
▶ 3 parts (1½ fl oz/45 ml) vodka
▶ 2 parts (1 fl oz/30 ml) fresh apple juice

you will also need
▶ Ice cubes
▶ Pomegranate seeds

bar tools
▶ Stemmed cocktail glass
▶ Muddler
▶ Cocktail shaker
▶ Strainer

Cost ♈♈
Degree of difficulty

preparation In advance: Chill the glass.

mixing Muddle the pomegranate seeds with the sugar in the shaker cup. Add the vodka and apple juice and shake briskly with ice. Strain into the glass.

garnish Garnish with pomegranate seeds.

Eden

This cocktail bursts with feel-good factors. Let's look at the name, for a start. Eden—"a place or state of unspoiled happiness or beauty." Doesn't that sound wonderful? The magic ingredient is rose syrup, made from fragrant rose petals. It has a delicate flavor, and an exotic aroma that takes you straight to that mystical place—it is the scent of Turkish Delight, the soft, sensuous Middle Eastern confection that melts in your mouth. Feel-good words—feel-good cocktail! Enjoy!

Like this? Try this
▶ **Negroni,** *page 113*

mixing ingredients
▶ 4 parts (2 fl oz/60 ml) gin
▶ 1 part (½ fl oz/15 ml) Campari®
▶ 2 parts (1 fl oz/30 ml) freshly squeezed lemon juice
▶ 1 part (½ fl oz/15 ml) rose syrup

you will also need
▶ Ice cubes
▶ Maraschino cherry

bar tools
▶ Lowball glass
▶ Bar spoon

Cost **YY**
Degree of difficulty

preparation In advance: Chill the glass.

mixing Stir the ingredients with ice in the glass.

garnish Garnish with a maraschino cherry.

Margarita

A great cocktail, and the first to be made with tequila—but are you wondering about the identity of the lady for whom the drink was named? There are several possibilities, the most plausible being that she was a wealthy Texan socialite, Margaret ("Margarita") Sames, whose friends dared her to invent a new drink during a Christmas party at her Acapulco home in 1948. She is also credited with garnishing the cocktail glass with a rim of coarse salt, thus transforming into one smooth action the tequila-drinker's tradition of licking salt, sipping tequila, and biting into a lime.

mixing ingredients
▸ 3 parts (1½ fl oz/45 ml) tequila (100 percent agave)
▸ 1½ parts (¾ fl oz/22.5 ml) freshly squeezed lime juice
▸ 1½ parts (¾ fl oz/22.5 ml) agave syrup
▸ 1½ parts (¾ fl oz/22.5 ml) still mineral water

you will also need
▸ Ice cubes
▸ Lime wedge (optional)
▸ Coarse salt (optional)
▸ Lime slice

bar tools
▸ Margarita or stemmed cocktail glass
▸ Cocktail shaker
▸ Strainer

Cost 🍸🍸
Degree of difficulty 🍹🍹

Like this? Try this
▸ **Frozen Margaritas,**
page 131

preparation In advance: Chill the glass. (Optional: Just before serving, scatter some salt on a paper towel. Rub the lime wedge around the rim of the glass, then dip the rim into the salt.)

mixing Shake the ingredients briskly with ice. Strain into the glass, taking care not to disturb the salt rim, if prepared.

garnish Garnish with a lime slice.

Like this? Try this
▶ **Blue Shark,** *page 58*

Blue Margarita

"Blue" can be a word with gloomy connotations. Even the most cheerful among us might be heard to say "I'm feeling a bit blue" on those less-than-perfect days, while Blues singers are doomed to be attached to their misery for ever. When it comes to love, however, blue can go either way: "I'm bluer than blue champagne" is a line from a 1940s song mourning a parting of the ways, while a blue moon is unreservedly romantic. So this gorgeous Blue Margarita can go with whatever mood you're in…

mixing ingredients
▶ 3 parts (1½ fl oz/45 ml) tequila
▶ 2 parts (1 fl oz/30 ml) blue curaçao
▶ 2 parts (1 fl oz/30 ml) freshly squeezed lime juice

you will also need
▶ Ice cubes
▶ Coarse salt
▶ Lime wedge
▶ Lemon and lime wedges

bar tools
▶ Stemmed cocktail glass
▶ Cocktail shaker
▶ Strainer

Cost ♉♉
Degree of difficulty

preparation In advance: Chill the glass. Just before serving, scatter some salt on a paper towel. Rub the lime wedge around the rim of the glass, then dip the rim into the salt.

mixing Shake the ingredients briskly with ice. Strain into the glass.

garnish Garnish with lemon and lime wedges.

Bronx

According to A.S. Crockett, historian of the Waldorf in New York and author of the *Old Waldorf-Astoria Bar Book*, published in 1935 and still in print, the Bronx cocktail was created around 1900 by the hotel's bartender, Johnnie Solon. It's essentially a perfect martini (that's a martini made with equal measures of sweet and dry vermouth), but with some freshly squeezed orange juice thrown in too. Solon—who was, allegedly, a teetotaler with a knack for mixing cocktails—obviously had the health of his customers in mind when he created this!

preparation In advance: Chill the glass.

mixing Shake the ingredients briskly with ice. Strain into the glass.

garnish Garnish with an orange slice and a maraschino cherry.

mixing ingredients
▶ 3 parts (1½ fl oz/45 ml) gin
▶ ½ tablespoon sweet vermouth
▶ ½ tablespoon dry vermouth
▶ 2 parts (1 fl oz/30 ml) freshly squeezed orange juice

you will also need
▶ Ice cubes
▶ Orange slice
▶ Maraschino cherry

bar tools
▶ Lowball glass
▶ Cocktail shaker
▶ Strainer

Like this? Try this
▶ **Gin Sling,** *page 105*

Cost **YYY**
Degree of difficulty

Old Fashioned

Don't you think there's something solid and comforting about a cocktail called an "Old Fashioned"? It has a charming air of a bewhiskered colonel about it. This is appropriate, actually, since it's claimed that it originated in the 1880s at a gentlemen's club, the Pendennis, in Louisville, Kentucky, and was popularized by one of its members, Colonel James E. Pepper. The Old Fashioned is one of the six basic cocktails listed in the 1948 classic work, *The Fine Art of Mixing Drinks*. Such a solid and comforting title for a book, too...

mixing ingredients
▸ 1 sugar cube
▸ 2 dashes Angostura® bitters
▸ 1 orange slice
▸ 4 parts (2 fl oz/60 ml) your favorite whiskey

you will also need
▸ Ice cubes
▸ Orange slice
▸ Maraschino cherries

bar tools
▸ Lowball glass
▸ Muddler
▸ Bar spoon

Cost ♈♈
Degree of difficulty

preparation In advance: Chill the glass.

mixing Soak the sugar cube with the Angostura® bitters in the glass, drop in the orange slice and muddle vigorously. Add some ice cubes and half the whiskey and stir. Top up with more ice cubes and the remaining whiskey.

garnish Garnish with maraschino cherries.

Like this? Try this
▸ **Whiskey Sour,** *page 57*

Cowboy Hoof

This is a variation on the Detroit Martini—which, made with vodka not gin, is without doubt a most appetizing cocktail. But let's face it—doesn't something called a Cowboy Hoof offer far more appeal to the imagination? You could get a few friends together, serve up a few of these, and spend a whole evening trying to work out where that name came from. Shall we give you a little clue? Well, it's—no, on second thoughts, that would spoil your fun...

mixing ingredients
▸ 1½ parts (1½ fl oz/45 ml) gin
▸ ½ teaspoon sugar syrup
▸ 1 dash orange bitters
▸ fresh mint sprig

you will also need
▸ Ice cubes
▸ Mint leaf
▸ Green olives

bar tools
▸ Stemmed cocktail glass
▸ Cocktail shaker
▸ Strainer

Cost ΥΥ
Degree of difficulty 🍊🍊

preparation In advance: Chill the glass.

mixing Shake the ingredients briskly with ice. Strain into the glass.

garnish Garnish with a mint leaf and green olives.

Like this? Try this
▸ **Campari Lady,**
page 113

Gimlet

Where the juice of a citrus fruit—lemon, orange, or lime—is called for in a cocktail recipe, it's nearly always best to get out the citrus press and squeeze. In the case of the Gimlet, however, you do it the easy way. No sticky fingers, no dishwashing—just remove the lid from a bottle of sweetened lime juice and you're away! The British brand "Rose's" is specified so often in association with the Gimlet that it seems likely the company itself invented the cocktail, to showcase their product. They got that right!

preparation In advance: Chill the glass.

mixing Strain over ice in the glass.

garnish Garnish with the lime wedges.

mixing ingredients
▶ 4 parts (2 fl oz/60 ml) gin
▶ 1 part (½ oz/15 ml) sweetened lime juice

you will also need
▶ Ice cubes
▶ Lime wedges

bar tools
▶ Stemmed cocktail glass
▶ Cocktail shaker
▶ Strainer

Cost ΥΥ
Degree of difficulty

Like this? Try this
▶ **City Rickey,** *page 101*

Daiquiri

This is a cocktail that, unusually, becomes *easier* to pronounce after you've drunk one or two. In Cuba, where it originated, they say "daiki-ri." Anywhere else, just let "da-kri" tumble off your tongue, and you'll be served an uncomplicated cocktail of white rum and lime juice, with just a touch of sugar—deliciously sour. Introduced to the States in 1909 by Admiral Lucius Johnson of the US Navy, the daiquiri enjoyed only quiet success at first. But 1940s' wartime rationing meant you couldn't get hold of the usual cocktail ingredients for love nor money, while Roosevelt's Good Neighbor policy made Cuban rum easy to come by—and suddenly a new star was born.

mixing ingredients
▶ 4 parts (2 fl oz/60 ml) white rum
▶ 2 parts (1 fl oz/30 ml) freshly squeezed lime juice
▶ 1 teaspoon superfine sugar (or substitute 1 tablespoon orange liqueur)

you will also need
▶ Ice cubes
▶ Lemon or orange slice

bar tools
▶ Stemmed cocktail glass
▶ Cocktail shaker
▶ Strainer

Cost ΥΥ
Degree of difficulty ◉◉

preparation In advance: Chill the glass.

mixing Shake the ingredients briskly with ice. Strain into the glass.

garnish Garnish with a lemon slice or an orange slice if using orange liqueur.

Like this? Try this
▶ **Strawberry Daiquiri,**
page 160

Blue Lady

To make a White Lady blue, you simply replace the Cointreau® with blue curaçao. Cointreau® is flavored with a blend of sweet and bitter orange peels. Blue curaçao is quite similar, but the orange flavor comes from the peel of the lahara citrus fruit, grown on the island of Curaçao. Oh, and blue curaçao is—*blue*.

mixing ingredients
▸ 3 parts (1½ fl oz/45 ml) gin
▸ 1½ parts (¾ fl oz/22.5 ml) blue curaçao
▸ 1½ parts (¾ fl oz/22.5 ml) freshly squeezed lemon juice

you will also need
▸ Ice cubes
▸ Maraschino cherry

bar tools
▸ Stemmed cocktail glass
▸ Cocktail shaker
▸ Strainer

Cost **YY**
Degree of difficulty 🏵🏵

preparation In advance: Chill the glass.

mixing Shake the ingredients briskly with ice. Strain into the glass.

garnish Garnish with a maraschino cherry.

Perfect Lady

Gentlemen everywhere, be very careful how you ask for this cocktail, especially if your lady is standing beside you at the time. "I'd like a Perfect Lady" is probably best avoided, while "Mine's a Perfect Lady" will almost certainly gain you plenty of points with your beloved.

mixing ingredients
▸ 3 parts (1½ fl oz/45 ml) gin
▸ 1½ parts (¾ fl oz/22.5 ml) peach brandy
▸ 1½ parts (¾ fl oz/22.5 ml) freshly squeezed lemon juice
▸ 1 tablespoon egg white

you will also need
▸ Ice cubes
▸ Lime spiral

bar tools
▸ Stemmed cocktail glass
▸ Cocktail shaker
▸ Strainer

Cost **YY**
Degree of difficulty 🏵🏵

preparation In advance: Chill the glass.

mixing Shake the ingredients briskly with ice. Strain into the glass.

garnish Garnish with a lime spiral.

White Lady

The White Lady claims to be the product of an early phase in the life of Harry MacElhone, before he opened his now legendary New York Bar in Paris. In 1919 he was bartender at the chic Ciro's Club in London, and this was where he invented the first incarnation of this cocktail, an alarming concoction of Cointreau®, crème de menthe, and lemon juice. With a further ten years' experience under Harry's belt, and his Parisian bar up and running, the original White Lady became a little more refined…

preparation In advance: Chill the glass.

mixing Shake the ingredients briskly with ice. Strain into the glass.

garnish Garnish with a lime spiral.

mixing ingredients
▸ 3 parts (1½ fl oz/45 ml) gin
▸ 1½ parts (¾ fl oz/22.5 ml) Cointreau®
▸ 1½ parts (¾ fl oz/22.5 ml) freshly squeezed lemon juice
▸ 1 tablespoon egg white (optional)

you will also need
▸ Ice cubes
▸ Lime spiral

bar tools
▸ Stemmed cocktail glass
▸ Cocktail shaker
▸ Strainer

Cost ▼▼
Degree of difficulty ●●

Like this? Try this
▸ **Singapore Sling**, *page 104*

Kyoto

To find the origin of the name of this cocktail, we have to look at one of the ingredients, melon liqueur. There are now several brands of this uncompromisingly green, syrupy but quite delicious liqueur on the market, but the very first incarnation was Midori®, created for a Japanese company with a brewery and distillery in Kyoto. Midori was famously launched in 1978 at New York's Studio 54, at the wrap party for the movie *Saturday Night Fever*. "Midori," by the way, is Japanese for "green." They're not kidding!

preparation In advance: Chill the glass.

mixing Shake the ingredients briskly with ice. Strain into the glass.

garnish Garnish with marinated pearl onions on a cocktail pick.

Like this? Try this
▸ **Appletini,** *page 130*

mixing ingredients
▸ 3 parts (1½ fl oz/45 ml) gin
▸ 1½ parts (¾ fl oz/22.5 ml) melon liqueur
▸ ¼ part (¼ fl oz/7.5 ml) dry vermouth
▸ ¼ teaspoon freshly squeezed lemon juice

you will also need
▸ Ice cubes
▸ Marinated pearl onions
▸ Decorative cocktail pick

bar tools
▸ Stemmed cocktail glass
▸ Cocktail shaker
▸ Strainer

Cost ￥￥￥
Degree of difficulty

mixing ingredients
▶ 3 parts (1½ fl oz/45 ml) pisco (40 percent)
▶ 2 parts (1 fl oz/30 ml) freshly squeezed lime juice
▶ 1 part (½ fl oz/15 ml) sugar syrup
▶ 1 tablespoon egg white

you will also need
▶ Ice cubes
▶ Angostura® bitters

bar tools
▶ Lowball glass
▶ Cocktail shaker
▶ Strainer

Cost ¥¥
Degree of difficulty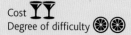

Pisco Sour

Pisco, a white brandy, is the national drink of Peru, and the Peruvians are very proud of it. It was introduced by Spanish invaders in the 16th century and shares its name with the port of Pisco, where the freedom fighter José de San Martin landed in 1820 and saw off the Spanish—which seems a little ungrateful!

preparation In advance: Chill the glass.

mixing Shake the ingredients briskly with ice. Strain over ice in the glass.

garnish Garnish with a few drops of Angostura® bitters.

mixing ingredients
▶ 4 parts (2 fl oz/60 ml) melon liqueur
▶ 1½ parts (¾ fl oz/22.5 ml) freshly squeezed lemon juice
▶ 1 teaspoon sugar
▶ 1 tablespoon juice from a jar of maraschino cherries

you will also need
▶ Ice cubes
▶ Maraschino cherry

bar tools
▶ Lowball glass
▶ Cocktail shaker
▶ Strainer

Cost ¥¥
Degree of difficulty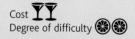

Midori Sour

There are lots of different ways to make a Midori Sour, but this one is really good fun—once you've got over the initial impression that the sun is setting in a startling green sky. Unless you have a very sweet tooth, you'll need every drop of that lemon juice to balance the flavor...

preparation In advance: Chill the glass.

mixing Shake the melon liqueur, lemon juice, and sugar briskly with ice. Pour the cherry juice over ice in the glass, then strain the mixed ingredients into the glass.

garnish Garnish with a maraschino cherry.

Whiskey Sour

A whiskey sour, made with bourbon, is one of the classics. Add a dash of egg white to the recipe to make a Boston Sour. For a Ward 8, use a mixture of lemon and orange juice, replace the sugar with grenadine syrup, and garnish with a miniature paper Massachusetts flag. Why the garnish? Because the cocktail was created in honor of Democrat Martin M. Lomasney who, in 1898, was elected to the General Court of Massachusetts, gaining the winning margin in Boston's Ward 8. There's a logic to everything...

mixing ingredients
▸ 3 parts (1½ fl oz/45 ml) bourbon whiskey
▸ 2 parts (1 fl oz/30 ml) freshly squeezed lemon juice
▸ 1 part (½ fl oz/15 ml) sugar syrup

you will also need
▸ Ice cubes
▸ Strip of lemon peel

bar tools
▸ Lowball glass
▸ Cocktail shaker
▸ Strainer

Cost **YY**
Degree of difficulty 🍊🍊

preparation In advance: Chill the glass.

mixing Shake the ingredients briskly with ice. Strain over ice in the glass.

garnish Garnish with a strip of lemon peel.

Like this? Try this
▸ **John Collins,**
page 106

Like this?
Try this
▸ **Blue Hawaii,**
page 96

mixing ingredients

▸ 1½ parts (¾ fl oz/22.5 ml) vodka
▸ ½ part (½ fl oz/15 ml) white tequila
▸ ½ part (½ fl oz/15 ml) blue curaçao

you will also need

▸ Cracked ice

bar tools

▸ Stemmed cocktail glass
▸ Cocktail shaker
▸ Strainer

Cost ♉♉♉
Degree of difficulty

Blue Shark

A Blue Shark is one of many variations on the Shark Bite, so called because—it bites! Not for the squeamish, a Bloody Shark Bite is made of dark rum with cranberry and orange juice, and a Great White Shark Attack is white rum with coconut milk, pineapple, and a drizzle of slightly *too* realistic raspberry liqueur. If, however, you're of a nervous disposition, try the Toothless Shark—it's just orange juice, grenadine, and lime juice, and will give you no more than an affectionate nibble...

preparation In advance: Chill the glass.

mixing Shake the ingredients briskly with ice. Strain into the glass.

Bramble

If you thought "I need my fix of ... " was a 21st-century expression, think again. This cocktail is a modern version of a Gin Fix, which appeared in the first edition of Jerry Thomas's *Bar-tender's Guide*, published in 1862—he clearly knew the value of a little bit of what you fancy! Jerry's Fix was made with raspberry syrup—if you can't find blackberry liqueur (which is sometimes seen as crème de mûre), use raspberry instead, or treat yourself to a bottle of Chambord® and enjoy a taste of both. Bramble heaven!

mixing ingredients
▶ 3 parts (1½ fl oz/45 ml) gin
▶ 1½ parts (½ fl oz/22.5 ml) freshly squeezed lemon juice
▶ 1 part (½ fl oz/15 ml) sugar syrup
▶ 1½ parts (¾ fl oz/22.5 ml) blackberry liqueur

you will also need
▶ Cracked ice
▶ Blackberries
▶ Lemon wedge

bar tools
▶ Lowball glass
▶ Bar spoon

Cost 🍸🍸
Degree of difficulty 🍊

preparation In advance: Chill the glass.

mixing Pour the gin, lemon juice, and sugar syrup over cracked ice in the glass. Stir, then slowly pour over the blackberry liqueur without stirring.

garnish Garnish with blackberries and a lemon wedge.

Like this? Try this
▶ **Black Bird,** *page 31*

3

After-dinner drinks

Irish Coffee

Irish coffee is surely the best way ever to end a special meal—it looks great and tastes even better. But coffee is just coffee, right? So what makes it Irish? Well, this way of serving it originated in the port town of Foynes in County Limerick, Ireland, when a head chef, Joseph Sheridan, took pity on a party of American passengers who arrived there on an inclement winter's evening back in the 1940s and added a generous slug of Irish whiskey to their coffee to warm them up. The layer of heavy cream is a must, but resist the urge to stir it in—you drink the coffee *through* the cream.

preparation In advance: Warm the glass. Make the coffee.

mixing Pour the coffee into the glass and stir in the sugar, then the whiskey. Carefully pour in the cream over the back of the spoon to form a thick layer on top of the coffee.

garnish Sprinkle with freshly grated nutmeg if you wish.

mixing ingredients
▸ 8 parts (4 fl oz/120 ml) strong hot black coffee, freshly made
▸ 1 teaspoon demerara sugar
▸ 4 parts (2 fl oz/60 ml) Irish whiskey
▸ 4 parts (2 fl oz/60 ml) heavy cream

you will also need
▸ Freshly grated nutmeg (optional)

bar tools
▸ Heatproof glass with a handle
▸ Bar spoon

Cost ΥΥ
Degree of difficulty ✹✹

Like this? Try this
▸ **Chocolate Cappuccino Martini,** *page 81*

Captain's Coffee

The "captain" for whom this cocktail is named was Sir Henry Morgan, an infamous Welsh privateer who sailed the Spanish Main in the 1600s, plundering and murdering and generally causing much havoc, while still managing to get himself appointed Lieutenant-Governor of Jamaica, albeit briefly. Today, the name of this notoriously wicked pirate lives on in the Captain Morgan Rum Company, whose range includes a spiced rum that the old Captain—a man who liked a drink—would no doubt have applauded.

mixing ingredients
▸ 2 parts (1 fl oz/30 ml) spiced rum
▸ 2 parts (1 fl oz/30 ml) coffee liqueur
▸ 1 dash Angostura® bitters

you will also need
▸ Ice cubes

bar tools
▸ Lowball glass
▸ Cocktail shaker
▸ Strainer

Cost
Degree of difficulty ✺✺

preparation In advance: Chill the glass.

mixing Shake the ingredients briskly with ice. Strain over ice in the glass.

Like this? Try this
▸ **Jamaican Sunset,**
page 134

Carrot Cake Shot

How crazy is this? A cocktail shot that tastes—even looks—like a slice of carrot cake! And great news for wheat allergy sufferers, there's not even a hint of gluten. So if you don't mind the fact that your favorite dessert is a little more liquid than usual, and has to be served in a glass, you can float away on a little fluffy cloud to carrot cake heaven. Leave out the cinnamon schnapps if you absolutely must, but you'll miss out on that evocative spicy aroma.

preparation In advance: Chill the glass and the spoon.

mixing Pour the Irish Cream into the glass. Very slowly pour in the butterscotch schnapps over the back of the spoon. Finally, drizzle in the cinnamon schnapps, if using.

mixing ingredients
▶ 1 part (½ fl oz/15 ml) Irish Cream
▶ 1 part (½ fl oz/15 ml) butterscotch schnapps
▶ 1 teaspoon cinnamon schnapps (optional)

bar tools
▶ Shot glass
▶ Bar spoon

Cost ♈♈
Degree of difficulty ✺✺✺

Like this? Try this
▶ **B-52,** *page 72*

Brandy Alexander

The original Alexander is a cocktail of gin, chocolate liqueur, and cream. The "Alexander" in question was the bartender of Rector's, a famous restaurant in pre-Prohibition New York, and it is thought that he invented the cocktail to serve at a dinner in honor of "Phoebe Snow," the fictional star of a railroad advertising campaign, who always wore white. The Brandy Alexander (or the Alexandra, made with ice cream instead of cream) rolls your dessert and after-dinner drink into one delectable concoction.

mixing ingredients
▸ 3 parts (1½ fl oz/45 ml) brandy
▸ 2 parts (1 fl oz/30 ml) white or dark crème de cacao
▸ 3 parts (1½ fl oz/45 ml) half-and-half cream

you will also need
▸ Ice cubes
▸ Freshly grated nutmeg

bar tools
▸ Stemmed cocktail glass
▸ Cocktail shaker
▸ Strainer

Cost 🍷🍷
Degree of difficulty 🍊🍊

preparation In advance: Chill the glass.

mixing Half-fill the shaker with ice cubes. Shake the ingredients briskly. Strain into the glass.

garnish Garnish with a sprinkling of freshly grated nutmeg.

Like this? Try this
▸ **Eggnog,** *page 187*

Brandy-Apricot Cocktail

Brandy, the classic after-dinner drink, is produced by distilling wine made from fermented grape juice. There are also fruit brandies, made from other fermented fruits. So what is the point of a Brandy Apricot Cocktail, when you could simply drink apricot brandy? Well, here's the difference—it's made with apricot liqueur, which isn't quite the same as apricot brandy because it's made, not from fermented apricot juice, but from apricot flesh and pits. Are you thoroughly confused now? Never mind, you only really need to know that it's a delicious digestif!

mixing ingredients
▶ 2 parts (1 fl oz/30 ml) brandy
▶ 1 part (½ fl oz/15 ml) apricot liqueur
▶ 1 part (½ fl oz/15 ml) freshly squeezed orange juice
▶ 1 part (½ fl oz/15 ml) freshly squeezed lemon juice

you will also need
▶ Ice cubes

bar tools
▶ Stemmed cocktail glass
▶ Cocktail shaker
▶ Strainer

Cost ♟♟
Degree of difficulty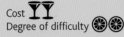

preparation In advance:
Chill the glass.

mixing Shake the ingredients briskly with ice. Strain into the glass.

Like this? Try this
▶ **Serbian Sidecar,** page 89

Brandy-Pepper Cocktail

This delectable cocktail sometimes goes by the name of "The Devil." Take a quick glance at the ingredients and you'll probably wonder what can possibly be so devilish about a brandy/crème de menthe combo. Sounds completely innocent, doesn't it? Now take a look at the garnish, and you'll find the fire...

preparation In advance: Chill the glass.

mixing Shake the ingredients briskly with ice. Strain into the glass.

Garnish Garnish with a pinch of cayenne pepper and a small red chili.

mixing ingredients
▸ 4 parts (2 fl oz/60 ml) brandy
▸ 2 parts (1 fl oz/30 ml) white crème de menthe

you will also need
▸ Ice cubes
▸ Pinch of cayenne pepper
▸ Small red chili

bar tools
▸ Stemmed cocktail glass
▸ Cocktail shaker
▸ Strainer

Cost ▮▮
Degree of difficulty 🍊🍊

French Connection

This after-dinner classic is simplicity itself. In order for it to have a French connection (as opposed to a Spanish connection, for example), it must be made with cognac, the world's most distinguished brandy, produced in the brandy region around the town of Cognac in southwest France. But as there's an equal measure of amaretto in this cocktail, shouldn't it be called a "Fritalian Connection" or maybe an "Itench Connection"?

preparation In advance: Chill the glass.

mixing Pour the ingredients over ice in the glass and stir gently.

mixing ingredients
▸ 2 parts (1 fl oz/30 ml) cognac (French brandy)
▸ 2 parts (1 fl oz/30 ml) amaretto

you will also need
▸ Ice cubes

bar tools
▸ Lowball glass
▸ Cocktail stirrer

Cost ▮▮
Degree of difficulty

Sombrero

You might need to practice this one a few times—it's not a Sombrero if you don't achieve the hat effect! The trick is to make it upside down, as it were, pouring the cream into the glass first, then slowly adding the Kahlúa®, which will sink through the cream and settle at the bottom of the glass. That's what's supposed to happen, anyway...

mixing ingredients
▸ 2 parts (1 fl oz/30 ml) light cream
▸ 2 parts (1 fl oz/30 ml) Kahlúa® (Mexican coffee liqueur)

bar tools
▸ Small tumbler

Cost ♉♉
Degree of difficulty ✹✹✹

mixing Pour the cream into the tumbler. Slowly and carefully pour the coffee liqueur through the cream.

Like this? Try this
▸ **White Russian,** *page 76*

Like this? Try this
▶ **White Cloud,**
page 163

Barbara

This after-dinner delight is smooth, creamy, and pure white. Well, after all, what else would you expect from a cocktail that is named in honor not of a mere person, but of a saint, Santa Barbara. But the color is where the symbolism comes to an abrupt end, because there's more than a touch of wickedness in here—it starts with the garnish of grated dark chocolate and goes on to embrace the vodka, disguised beneath its pale cloak of white crème de cacao...

preparation In advance: Chill the glass.

mixing Shake the ingredients briskly with ice. Strain into the glass.

garnish Garnish with grated dark chocolate.

mixing ingredients
▶ 2 parts (1 fl oz/30 ml) vodka
▶ 1 part (½ fl oz/15 ml) white crème de cacao
▶ 1 part (½ fl oz/15 ml) light cream

you will also need
▶ Ice cubes
▶ Grated dark chocolate

bar tools
▶ Stemmed cocktail glass
▶ Cocktail shaker
▶ Strainer

Cost 🍸🍸
Degree of difficulty 🔘🔘

B-52

This spectacular cocktail shooter needs a steady hand, a little confidence, and a lot of faith—the ingredients cannot fail to layer because of their differences in specific gravity, but you might need to make a few before you're convinced! The drink is named after the Air Force's B-52 Stratofortress long-range bomber—and it hits the spot—while a Flaming B-52, a slightly hazardous variation of this cocktail, does a mean imitation of the incendiary bombs released by the plane.

mixing ingredients
▸ 1 part (½ fl oz/15 ml) coffee liqueur
▸ 1 part (½ fl oz/15 ml) Amarula® or Irish Cream
▸ 1 part (½ fl oz/15 ml) Grand Marnier®

bar tools
▸ Shot glass
▸ Bar spoon

Cost ♈♈♈
Degree of difficulty ✺✺✺

preparation In advance: Chill the glass and the spoon.

mixing Pour the coffee liqueur into the glass. Very slowly pour in the Amarula® or Irish Cream over the back of the spoon. Very slowly pour in the Grand Marnier® over the back of the spoon.

Like this? Try this
▸ **Carrot Cake Shot,** page 65

B-57

Like the B-52, this shot is named after a bomber, the B-57 Canberra. The difference between a B-52 and a B-57 (the cocktails, not the bombers) is that the B-57 is made with sambuca, an Italian aniseed-flavor liqueur, instead of Amarula® or Irish Cream. Aniseed is one of those things you love or hate, so decide how you feel about it *before* you try this!

preparation In advance: Chill the glass and the spoon.

mixing Pour the coffee liqueur into the glass. Very slowly pour in the triple sec over the back of the spoon. Very slowly pour in the sambuca over the back of the spoon.

mixing ingredients
▶ 1 part (½ fl oz/15 ml) coffee liqueur
▶ 1 part (½ fl oz/15 ml) triple sec
▶ 1 part (½ fl oz/15 ml) sambuca

bar tools
▶ Shot glass
▶ Bar spoon

Cost ▮▮▮
Degree of difficulty ◉◉◉

B-61

Mozart would no doubt have been very proud to see his name on a bottle of delectable chocolate liqueur, although he might have wondered how something so sweet, delicious, and benign ended up in a cocktail named after the B61 nuclear bomb, which is anything but! He'd probably have been quite pleased, also, that we still enjoy his music so much…

preparation In advance: Chill the glass and the spoon.

mixing Pour the vanilla liqueur into the glass. Very slowly pour in the chocolate liqueur over the back of the spoon. Very slowly pour in the white rum over the back of the spoon.

mixing ingredients
▶ 1 part (½ fl oz/15 ml) vanilla liqueur
▶ 1 part (½ fl oz/15 ml) Mozart Gold Chocolate Liqueur®
▶ 1 part (½ fl oz/15 ml) white rum

bar tools
▶ Shot glass
▶ Bar spoon

Cost ▮▮▮
Degree of difficulty ◉◉◉

Grasshopper

The Grasshopper was created by Philip Guichet at Tujague's, a long-established restaurant and bar in the French Quarter of New Orleans, and won him a place as finalist in New York's Early Times National Mixed Drink Competition back in 1956. Its name derives from the delicate green color imparted by the crème de menthe, though you could find yourself hopping about from sheer enjoyment. And be warned—in an episode of *The Big Bang Theory* named "The Grasshopper Experiment, " a shy character becomes noticeably bolder after drinking a Grasshopper...

mixing ingredients
▶ 1½ parts (¾ fl oz/22.5 ml) green crème de menthe
▶ 1½ parts (¾ fl oz/22.5 ml) white crème de cacao
▶ 1½ parts (¾ fl oz/22.5 ml) light cream

you will also need
▶ Ice cubes
▶ Chocolate flakes

bar tools
▶ Stemmed cocktail glass
▶ Cocktail shaker
▶ Strainer

Cost ♈♈
Degree of difficulty ◉◉

preparation In advance: Chill the glass.

mixing Shake the ingredients briskly with ice. Strain into the glass.

garnish Garnish with chocolate flakes.

Like this? Try this
▶ **Russian Spring,**
page 149

Cockroach

A few words on the subject of the cockroach. These large insects like to hang out with people who have lovely warm homes, but as roomies they're not that great—they eat your food and leave an unpleasant smell. They invite their friends along and once they've all moved in they're usually keen to stay, no matter how firmly you ask them to leave. As for this cocktail, if you don't mind drinking something that's the same color as a cockroach and shares its name, it's really good!

mixing ingredients
▸ 1 part (½ fl oz/15 ml) coffee liqueur
▸ 1 part (½ fl oz/15 ml) whiskey liqueur

bar tools
▸ Shot glass
▸ Bar spoon

Cost **YY**

Degree of difficulty

---

preparation In advance: Chill the glass and the spoon.

mixing Pour the coffee liqueur into the glass. Very slowly pour in the whiskey liqueur over the back of the bar spoon.

Like this? Try this
▸ **Heather's Pleasure** *page 82*

White Russian

The White Russian isn't a traditional Russian drink—they'd probably be inclined to leave out the coffee liqueur and the cream, leaving only the vodka that puts the "Russian" into this cocktail. But what a romantic name, associated as it is with the anti-Bolshevik movement in the Russian Revolution, even though it almost certainly has nothing to do with that event... The White Russian had a new lease of life following the 1998 movie *The Big Lebowski*, in which it starred as the favorite drink of Jeffrey "the Dude."

mixing ingredients
▸ 4 parts (2 fl oz/60 ml) vodka
▸ 2 parts (1 fl oz/30 ml) coffee liqueur
▸ 2 parts (1 fl oz/30 ml) light cream

you will also need
▸ Ice cubes
▸ Maraschino cherries

bar tools
▸ Lowball glass
▸ Cocktail shaker
▸ Strainer

Cost 🍸🍸
Degree of difficulty 🍊🍊

preparation In advance: Chill the glass.

mixing Shake the vodka and coffee liqueur briskly with ice. Strain over ice in the glass, then pour in the cream.

garnish Garnish with a maraschino cherry.

Like this? Try this
▸ **Sombrero,** *page 70*

Black Russian

While the White Russian suggests noble causes, the Black Russian sounds positively sinister. In fact, there's nothing sinister about it at all—it was created in 1949 by a bartender at the Hotel Metropole in Brussels in honor of the newly appointed U.S. Ambassador to Luxembourg, Perle Mesta (who also, incidentally, inspired the Irving Berlin musical *Call Me Madam*).

preparation In advance: Chill the glass.

mixing Fill the glass with ice. Pour in the vodka, followed by the coffee liqueur.

mixing ingredients
▶ 4 parts (2 fl oz/60 ml) vodka
▶ 2 parts (1 fl oz/30 ml) coffee liqueur

you will also need
▶ Ice cubes

bar tools
▶ Lowball glass

Cost ▼▼
Degree of difficulty 🌑

Pink Russian

Your first thought on reading this was probably: "*Pink* Russian? Yeah, right!" But this member of the Russian family is tougher than it sounds—it's not just vodka and coffee liqueur, but tequila too. Yes, it's strawberry cream liqueur-flavored tequila, and therefore a bit on the pink side, but don't let that fool you...

preparation In advance: Chill the glass.

mixing Shake the ingredients briskly with ice. Strain over ice in the glass.

garnish Garnish with a strawberry.

mixing ingredients
▶ 2 parts (1 fl oz/30 ml) tequila strawberry cream liqueur
▶ 2 parts (1 fl oz/30 ml) coffee liqueur
▶ 1 part (½ fl oz/15 ml) vodka
▶ 1 part (½ fl oz/15 ml) milk

you will also need
▶ Ice cubes
▶ Strawberry

bar tools
▶ Highball glass
▶ Cocktail shaker
▶ Strainer

Cost ▼▼▼
Degree of difficulty 🌑🌑

American Beauty

This cocktail is named after the exquisite, deep-pink, scented rose "American Beauty," which was bred in France in 1875 by Henri Lédéchaux. The rose has also inspired a ragtime tune (*American Beauty Rag*, published in 1913 by Joseph Lamb); an album released in 1970 by the rock band Grateful Dead, which featured the rose on its cover; and a movie (*American Beauty*, premiered in 1999). So when you ask for an American Beauty, you take your chances on actually getting a drink!

mixing ingredients
- ▶ 2 parts (1 fl oz/30 ml) brandy
- ▶ 2 parts (1 fl oz/30 ml) dry vermouth
- ▶ 2 parts (1 fl oz/30 ml) freshly squeezed orange juice
- ▶ 1 teaspoon grenadine
- ▶ ¼ teaspoon white crème de menthe
- ▶ 1 part (½ fl oz/15 ml) port

you will also need
- ▶ Ice cubes

bar tools
- ▶ Lowball glass
- ▶ Cocktail shaker
- ▶ Strainer

Cost ￥￥￥
Degree of difficulty

preparation In advance: Chill the glass.

mixing Shake all the ingredients except the port briskly with ice. Strain into the glass and carefully pour in the port.

Like this? Try this
▶ **Brandy Alexander,**
page 66

Chocolatini

mixing ingredients
▸ 3 parts (1½ fl oz/45 ml) vanilla vodka
▸ 3 parts (1½ fl oz/45 ml) dark chocolate liqueur

you will also need
▸ Ice cubes

bar tools
▸ Stemmed cocktail glass
▸ Cocktail shaker
▸ Strainer

Cost **YY**
Degree of difficulty 🍊🍊

Chocoholics everywhere, your moment has arrived. The Chocolate Martini—which sounds even more attractive when you roll it into a Chocolatini—is just heaven. Before you commit your ingredients to the cocktail shaker, it's *absolutely essential* that you check out several brands of chocolate liqueur so that you can identify your favorite (all in the name of research, of course). Once you've done that, you might want to play around with the recipe a little—maybe vary the proportions of vodka to chocolate liqueur, perhaps add some chocolate sauce to the glass. Feel free to make up your own excuse to be greedy!

preparation In advance: Chill the glass.

mixing Shake the ingredients briskly with ice. Strain into the glass.

Like this?
Try this
▸ **B-61,** *page 73*

Chocolate Coffee Martini

If you want a coffee martini with only a hint of chocolate flavor, try adding a little pure chocolate extract. It has a deliciously intense taste but no alcohol, giving you the right to deny in wide-eyed indignation any accusations of over-indulgent behavior. You can, of course, use chocolate-flavor vodka—after all, who'll know?

preparation In advance: Chill the glass.

mixing Shake the ingredients briskly with ice. Strain into the glass.

mixing ingredients
▸ 4 parts (2 fl oz/60 ml) vodka or chocolate vodka
▸ 2 parts (1 fl oz/30 ml) coffee liqueur
▸ 1 teaspoon pure chocolate extract

you will also need
▸ Ice cubes

bar tools
▸ Stemmed cocktail glass
▸ Cocktail shaker
▸ Strainer

Cost ♟♟
Degree of difficulty

Chocolate Cappuccino Martini

You want this to look as much like a real cappuccino as possible, so shake, shake, shake the ingredients until they're really frothy and sprinkle your cocktail with your favorite garnish. Of course, the fact that you're drinking your cappuccino from a cocktail glass might be something of a giveaway...

preparation In advance: Chill the glass.

mixing Shake the ingredients briskly with ice. Strain into the glass.

garnish Sprinkle with your favorite garnish—powdered cinnamon or chocolate, or both!

mixing ingredients
▸ 2 parts (1 fl oz/30 ml) Irish Cream
▸ 2 parts (1 fl oz/30 ml) milk
▸ ½ tablespoon cappuccino liqueur
▸ ½ tablespoon white crème de cacao

you will also need
▸ Ice cubes
▸ Your favorite cappuccino garnish

bar tools
▸ Stemmed cocktail glass
▸ Cocktail shaker
▸ Strainer

Cost ♟♟♟
Degree of difficulty

Heather's Pleasure

mixing ingredients
▸ 2 parts (1 fl oz/30 ml) chocolate liqueur
▸ 2 parts (1 fl oz/30 ml) heather cream

bar tools
▸ Shot glass
▸ Bar spoon

Cost ŸŸ
Degree of difficulty 🍊🍊🍊

Don't worry if your name isn't Heather—you're not barred from drinking this cocktail. On the other hand, when you've tasted it, you might *want* to change your name to Heather, just for the joy of knowing that a delicious cocktail not only bears your name, but is also mindful of your pleasure! Heather cream, by the way, is a blend of single malt Scotch whisky and heavy cream. Unaccountably, it has a slight chocolate flavor, which works *so* well here...

preparation In advance: Chill the glass and the spoon.

mixing Pour the chocolate liqueur into the glass. Very slowly pour in the heather cream over the back of the bar spoon.

Like this? Try this
▸ **Cockroach,**
page 75

Like this? Try this
▶ **Banana Punch,**
page 128

White Heather

This cocktail should be made with Scotch whisky, because white heather is Scotland's traditional token of good luck. And here's why: Several hundred years ago, Malvina was engaged to Oscar, who went off in search of fame and fortune but was killed in battle. Malvina, upon hearing the news, ran hither and thither over a hill clad in purple heather, which turned white where her tears fell. And Malvina made a wish that the white heather would bring good fortune to all those who found it.

preparation In advance: Chill the glass.

mixing Shake the ingredients briskly with ice. Strain into the glass.

garnish Garnish with powdered cinnamon and a piece of cinnamon stick.

mixing ingredients
▶ 1 part (½ fl oz/15 ml) Scotch whisky
▶ 1 part (½ fl oz/15 ml) crème de banane
▶ 1 part (½ fl oz/15 ml) white crème de cacao
▶ 2 parts (1 fl oz/30 ml) light cream

you will also need
▶ Ice cubes
▶ Powdered cinnamon
▶ Cinnamon stick

bar tools
▶ Stemmed cocktail glass
▶ Cocktail shaker
▶ Strainer

Cost ♈♈♈
Degree of difficulty ◉◉

Green Dragon

There are several recipes for a Green Dragon—
however, this one has only two ingredients, one of which
is an elixir of long life, and not many cocktails can make
that claim! Green Chartreuse® has been made by
Carthusian monks in France since 1764 and is adapted
from a much older elixir recipe—at any one time, only
two monks know the identity of the 130 plants that
go into the liqueur. Mystery and intrigue in a glass!

mixing ingredients
▶ 4 parts (2 fl oz/60 ml) vodka
▶ 2 parts (1 fl oz/30 ml) green Chartreuse®

you will also need
▶ Ice cubes

bar tools
▶ Stemmed cocktail glass
▶ Cocktail shaker
▶ Strainer

Cost ⲎⲎ
Degree of difficulty

preparation
In advance: Chill the glass.

mixing
Shake the ingredients briskly
with ice. Strain into the glass.

Like this? Try this
▶ **Lemon Twist Martini,** *page 34*

Tricolor

We can say with confidence that most people love Italian food. So if you serve an Italian meal *and* follow it with this shooter layered with the colors of the Italian flag, your family/friends are going to think you are simply amazing! Absinthe (that's the green stripe) tastes of anise, but don't be put off if you don't like this flavor—it will soon be tempered by the freshness of lemon and the sweetness of grenadine…

preparation In advance: Chill the glass.

mixing Pour the grenadine into the glass. Very slowly pour in the lemon cream liqueur over the back of a bar spoon. Very slowly pour in the absinthe over the back of the bar spoon.

mixing ingredients
▶ 1 part (½ fl oz/15 ml) grenadine
▶ 1 part (½ fl oz/15 ml) lemon cream liqueur
▶ 1 part (½ fl oz/15 ml) absinthe

bar tools
▶ Shot glass
▶ Bar spoon

Cost ΥΥΥ
Degree of difficulty

Like this? Try this
▶ **Fireball Shot,** *page 90*

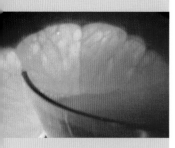

Creamsicle

What better way to round off a really special, thoroughly grown-up dinner than with a cocktail bearing the slightly absurd but nonetheless endearing name of "Creamsicle"? The name and the taste might recall your childhood, but the kick will soon remind you that those days are gone! A touch of vanilla is essential for the authentic creamsicle experience. Brandy lovers can make this with Tuaca® (vanilla-flavored brandy-based Italian liqueur) rather than vodka—the vanilla flavor really comes through and the color is just perfect for this strictly adults-only treat.

mixing ingredients
▸ 1 part (½ fl oz/15 ml) triple sec
▸ 1 part (½ fl oz/15 ml) vanilla vodka or Tuaca®
▸ 4 parts (2 fl oz/60 ml) freshly squeezed orange juice
▸ 2 parts (1 fl oz/30 ml) light cream

you will also need
▸ Ice cubes
▸ Orange slice

bar tools
▸ Stemmed cocktail glass
▸ Cocktail shaker
▸ Strainer

Cost 🍸🍸
Degree of difficulty ✹✹

preparation In advance: Chill the glass.

mixing Shake the ingredients briskly with ice. Strain into the glass.

garnish Garnish with an orange slice.

Like this? Try this
▸ **B-61,** *page 73*

Sidecar

mixing ingredients
▸ 2 parts (1 fl oz/30 ml) brandy
▸ 2 parts (1 fl oz/30 ml) orange liqueur
▸ 1½ parts (¾ fl oz/22.5 ml) freshly squeezed lemon juice

you will also need
▸ Ice cubes
▸ Sugar (optional)
▸ Lemon wedge (optional)

bar tools
▸ Stemmed cocktail glass
▸ Cocktail shaker
▸ Strainer

Cost ⏶⏶
Degree of difficulty ✹✹

When the New York Bar opened in Paris in 1911, it was an instant hit with American expats. A handful of years later, in 1923, it was acquired by a Scot, one Harry MacElhone, who renamed it Harry's New York Bar and—according to legend—invented the Sidecar. This elegant cocktail headed for the States when Prohibition ended, and there were those who declared it almost made those long, dry years worth the wait. Meanwhile, Harry's Bar—popular as ever—has dubbed itself "The oldest cocktail bar in Europe."

preparation In advance: Chill the glass. (Optional: Just before serving, scatter some sugar on a paper towel. Rub the lemon wedge around the rim of the glass, then dip the rim into the sugar.)

mixing Shake the ingredients briskly with ice. Strain into the glass, taking care not to disturb the sugar rim, if prepared.

Like this? Try this
▸ **Brandy-Apricot Cocktail,** page 68

Boston Sidecar

This cocktail appeared in the 1946 edition of the *Old Mr. Boston De Luxe Official Bartender's Guide* and, strictly speaking, it's only a genuine Boston Sidecar if you use Mr. Boston imported Virgin Islands rum. Confusingly, if you use lemon juice instead of lime it's called Between the Sheets! How did *that* happen?

preparation In advance: Chill the glass.

mixing Shake the ingredients briskly with ice. Strain into the glass.

mixing ingredients
▸ 1½ parts (¾ fl oz/ 22.5 ml) white rum
▸ 1½ parts (¾ fl oz/ 22.5 ml) brandy
▸ 1½ parts (¾ fl oz/ 22.5 ml) triple sec
▸ 1 part (½ fl oz/15 ml) freshly squeezed lime juice

you will also need
▸ Ice cubes

bar tools
▸ Stemmed cocktail glass
▸ Cocktail shaker
▸ Strainer

Cost ΥΥΥ
Degree of difficulty ⊛⊛

Serbian Sidecar

Plum brandy and orange liqueur are the perfect ingredients for a cocktail to serve during the Christmas holiday season. Slivovitz—plum brandy—is what transforms this into a Serbian Sidecar, though as this delicious drink is produced throughout eastern Europe it could equally be called a Slovakian Sidecar, a Bulgarian Sidecar, a Romanian Sidecar...

preparation In advance: Chill the glass.

mixing Shake the ingredients briskly with ice. Strain into the glass.

garnish Garnish with an orange slice.

mixing ingredients
▸ 2 parts (1 fl oz/30 ml) plum brandy
▸ 2 parts (1 fl oz/30 ml) orange liqueur
▸ 1½ parts (¾ fl oz/22.5 ml) freshly squeezed lemon juice

you will also need
▸ Ice cubes
▸ Orange slice

bar tools
▸ Stemmed cocktail glass
▸ Cocktail shaker
▸ Strainer

Cost ΥΥ
Degree of difficulty ⊛⊛

Fireball Shot

Goodness, gracious, great Fireball Shots! This one's a real "bad boy." The green layer is absinthe, once deemed so dangerous that it was banned in several countries for almost a hundred years—Van Gogh was reputedly in an absinthe haze when that unfortunate incident took place involving his left ear... Then there's the heat. Now, some people actually set light to their fireball shots, but that's just crazy. On the other hand, you might think that adding an unspecified quantity of habañero pepper sauce to your after-dinner drink is equally insane!

mixing ingredients
▸ 1 part (½ fl oz/15 ml) absinthe
▸ 1 part (½ fl oz/15 ml) red sambuca
▸ Tabasco® habañero pepper sauce to taste

bar tools
▸ Stemmed shot glass
▸ Bar spoon

Cost ♈♈
Degree of difficulty ⊛⊛⊛

preparation In advance: Chill the glass and the spoon.

mixing Pour the absinthe into the glass. Very slowly pour in the red sambuca over the back of a bar spoon and add the Tabasco® to taste, a drop at a time.

Like this? Try this
▸ **Brandy-Pepper Cocktail**
page 69

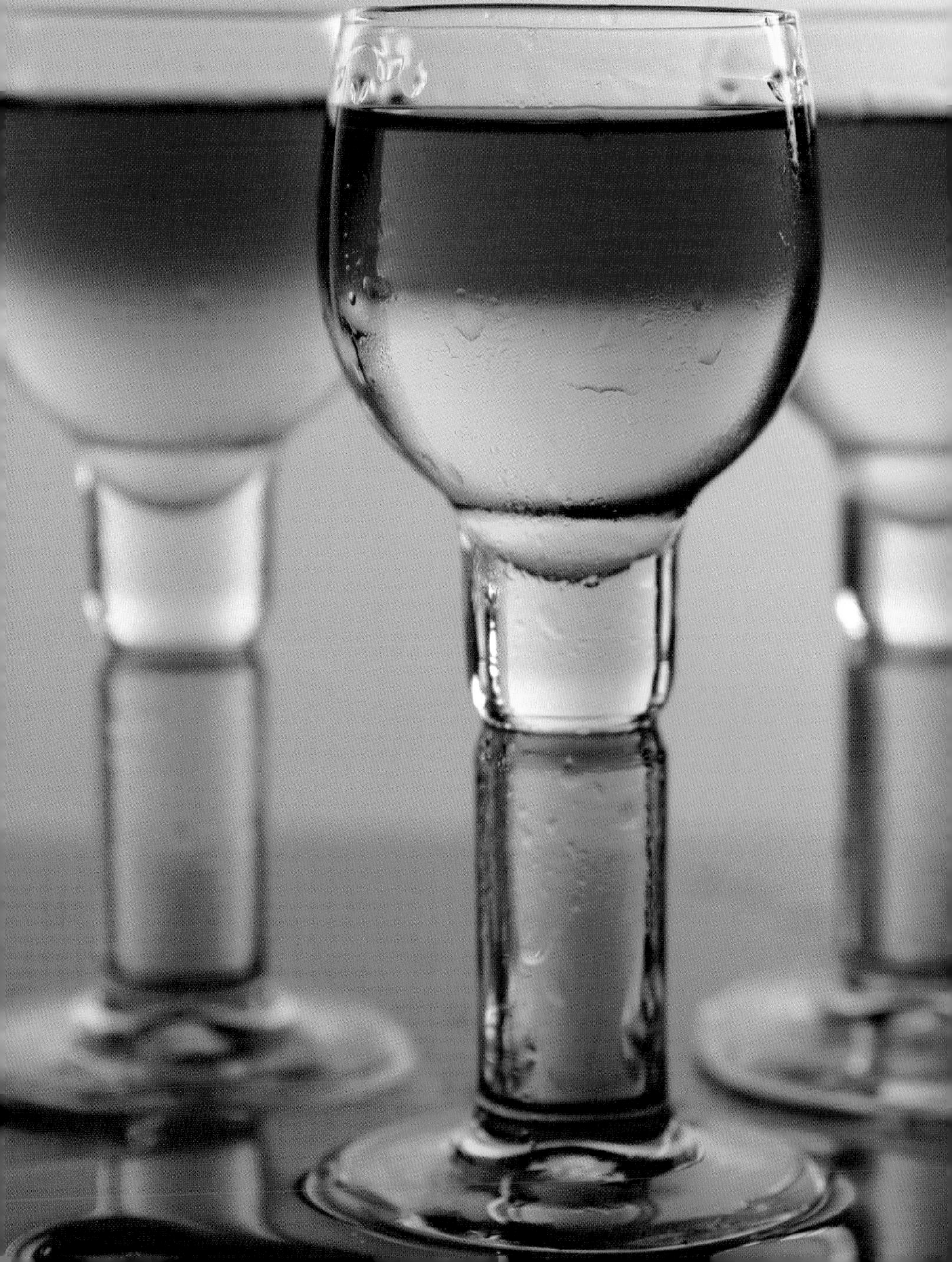

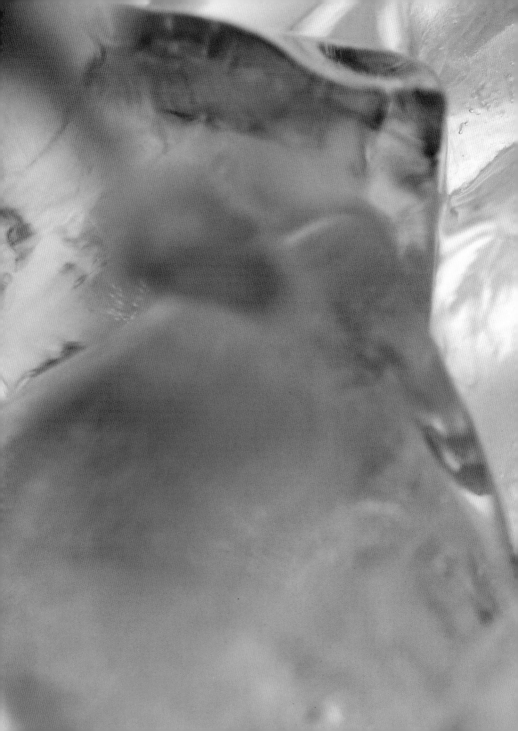

4

Long and Cool

Like this? Try this
▸ **Planter's Punch,**
page 129

Mai Tai

"Mai tai" is the Tahitian word for "good"—which seems something of an understatement when applied to the Mai Tai, a delectable combination of rum, curaçao, and lime. However, the story goes that, back in 1944, Victor J. Bergeron—the owner of Trader Vic's, a restaurant in Oakland, California—created the drink for some visiting friends from Tahiti. One of them took a sip and exclaimed with gusto: "Mai tai roa ae!" meaning "Out of this world!" Now, *that* is a far more accurate description ...

mixing ingredients
▸ 4 parts (2 fl oz/60 ml) gold rum
▸ 1 part (½ fl oz/15 ml) orange curaçao
▸ 2 parts (1 fl oz/30 ml) freshly squeezed lime juice
▸ 1 part (½ fl oz/15 ml) orgeat syrup
▸ 1 part (½ fl oz/15 ml) sugar syrup

you will also need (for all three versions)
▸ Ice cubes
▸ Pineapple wedge
▸ Maraschino cherry
▸ Cocktail umbrella

bar tools
▸ Highball glass
▸ Cocktail shaker
▸ Strainer

Cost Y Y
Degree of difficulty

preparation In advance: Chill the glass.

mixing Shake the ingredients briskly with ice. Strain over ice cubes in the glass.

garnish Garnish with a pineapple wedge, a maraschino cherry, and a cocktail umbrella.

Pineapple Mai Tai

This version of the Mai Tai is guaranteed to upset the purists, who will insist that it should never be made with pineapple juice, so the best idea is to make one for yourself (and perhaps a trusted friend), then enjoy it quietly in a secluded spot, far from the madding crowd—and those horrified purists...

preparation In advance: Chill the glass.

mixing Shake the ingredients briskly with ice. Strain over ice cubes in the glass.

garnish Garnish with a pineapple wedge, a maraschino cherry, and a cocktail umbrella.

mixing ingredients
- 1 part (½ fl oz/15 ml) dark rum
- 1 part (½ fl oz/15 ml) white rum
- 1 part (½ fl oz/15 ml) orange liqueur
- 4 parts (2 fl oz/60 ml) fresh pineapple juice
- 4 parts (2 fl oz/60 ml) freshly squeezed orange juice
- ½ part (¼ fl oz/7.5 ml) freshly squeezed lime juice
- 1 dash of grenadine

bar tools
See Mai Tai *page 94*

Cost ΥΥΥ
Degree of difficulty 🍊🍊

Strawberry Mai Tai

You can make this with strawberry liqueur, but when fresh strawberries are in season it's good to use those instead. Look out for an orgeat syrup made with rose water—the flavor marries really well with strawberries. In fact, this romantic union would make the Strawberry Mai Tai perfect to serve at a summer wedding ...

preparation In advance: Chill the glass. If using fresh strawberries, muddle them briskly with the sugar syrup in the mixing glass.

mixing Shake the ingredients briskly with ice. Strain over ice cubes in the glass.

garnish Garnish with a pineapple wedge, a maraschino cherry, and a cocktail umbrella.

mixing ingredients
- 4 parts (2 fl oz/60 ml) gold rum
- 1 part (½ fl oz/15 ml) orange liqueur
- 2 parts (1 fl oz/30 ml) freshly squeezed lime juice
- 1 part (½ fl oz/15 ml) orgeat syrup
- 1 part (½ fl oz/15 ml) strawberry liqueur OR
- 1 part (½ fl oz/15 ml) sugar syrup + two fresh strawberries, diced

bar tools
See Mai Tai *page 94*
- Muddler (optional)
- Mixing glass (optional)

Cost ΥΥΥ
Degree of difficulty 🍊🍊

Like this? Try this
▶ **Electric Lemonade,**
page 183

Blue Hawaii

In the late 1950s, a dazzling blue liqueur was launched that took cocktail-making to a whole new level of fun—blue curaçao. The producers found the perfect candidate for the job of creating a cocktail using the orange-flavored liqueur—Harry K. Yee, a bartender at the Hilton Hawaiian Village Beach Resort and Spa, Honolulu, whose motto was: "A Hawaiian drink to me is something they don't get back home." He is also credited with introducing garnishes such as cocktail umbrellas and flowers, those little touches that make a cocktail really special.

mixing ingredients
▶ 1½ parts (¾ fl oz/22.5 ml) vodka
▶ 1½ parts (¾ fl oz/22.5 ml) white rum
▶ 1 part (½ fl oz/15 ml) blue curaçao
▶ 6 parts (3 fl oz/90 ml) fresh pineapple juice
▶ 2 parts (1 fl oz/30 ml) sweet and sour mix

you will also need
▶ Ice cubes
▶ Orange slice
▶ Orchid or hibiscus flower (optional)

bar tools
▶ Highball or hurricane glass
▶ Cocktail shaker
▶ Strainer

Cost ¥¥¥
Degree of difficulty

preparation In advance: Chill the glass.

mixing Shake the ingredients briskly with ice. Strain into the glass.

garnish Garnish with an orange slice and a flower, if using.

Blue Lagoon

The Blue Lagoon was invented in 1960 at Harry's New York Bar in Paris by Harry's son, Andy. There's something of a "which came first, the name or the drink?" mystery about this cocktail—was the drink inspired by the romantic novel *The Blue Lagoon*, or did the glorious color of the drink inspire the name? By the way, to ring the changes—or if you simply prefer your lagoons green—replace the lemonade with pineapple juice.

preparation In advance: Chill the glass.

mixing Pour the vodka over ice in the glass, add the blue curaçao, top up with lemonade, and stir.

garnish Garnish with the wedge of orange and a cocktail umbrella.

mixing ingredients
▸ 2 parts (1 fl oz/30 ml) vodka
▸ 1 part (½ fl oz/15 ml) blue curaçao
▸ Lemonade, to top up

you will also need
▸ Ice cubes
▸ Orange wedge
▸ Cocktail umbrella

bar tools
▸ Highball or hurricane glass
▸ Bar spoon

Cost 🍸🍸
Degree of difficulty

Like this? Try this
▸ **Blue Lady,**
page 52

New York

mixing ingredients
▸ 4 parts (2 fl oz/60 ml)
Canadian whisky
▸ 1½ parts (¾ fl oz/22.5 ml)
fresh squeezed lime juice
▸ 1 part (½ fl oz/15 ml)
sugar syrup
▸ 1 teaspoon grenadine

you will also need
▸ Ice cubes
▸ Strip of orange peel,
knotted
▸ Maraschino cherry

bar tools
▸ Lowball glass
▸ Cocktail shaker
▸ Strainer

Cost **ΥΥ**
Degree of
difficulty 🍊🍊

It's inevitable that there's a cocktail called a "New York," because although the concept wasn't actually invented in the Big Apple, this city above all others is associated with it. In May 2006 an exhibition called "The Cocktail in New York" opened to celebrate the 200th anniversary of the first printed description (in *The Balance, and Columbian repository* of Hudson, N.Y.): "Cock tail, then, is a stimulating liquor composed of spirits of any kind, sugar, water, and bitters." Of course, the cocktail has come a long way since those unpromising words were published ...

preparation In advance: Chill the glass.

mixing Strain over ice in the glass.

garnish Garnish with an orange peel knot and a maraschino cherry.

Like this? Try this
▸ **Whiskey
Rickey,** *page 101*

Island Breeze

"Breeze" is a gentle, evocative word, and this is a gentle, evocative drink. Even the rum, made in the southern Caribbean Islands that inspired the name of this cocktail, is the most gentle of all the rums—light and delicate, both in body and flavor. Just close your eyes, take a sip, and you're there, with that soft breeze rippling the sea and whispering in the palm trees. What's that it's saying? Ah, yes: "Waiter! Another one, please..."

preparation In advance: Chill the glass.

mixing Fill the glass with ice. Add the ingredients one at a time.

garnish Garnish with lime wedges.

mixing ingredients
- 3 parts (1½ fl oz/45 ml) white rum
- 8 parts (4 fl oz/120 ml) fresh pineapple juice
- 2 parts (1 fl oz/30 ml) cranberry juice
- 2 dashes Angostura® bitters

you will also need
- Ice cubes
- Lime wedges

bar tools
- Highball glass

Cost **YY**
Degree of difficulty ✱

Like this? Try this
▸ **Sea Breeze,** *page 143*

mixing ingredients
▸ 3 parts (1½ fl oz/45 ml) gin
▸ 1 part (½ fl oz/15 ml) freshly squeezed lime juice
▸ club soda, to top up

you will also need
▸ Ice cubes
▸ Lime wedges

bar tools
▸ Highball glass
▸ Bar spoon

Cost ΥΥ
Degree of difficulty ✹

Gin Rickey

Colonel Joseph Karr Rickey, who died in 1903, achieved many things during his life. He fought in the US Confederate Army and was one of four famous colonels whose names were familiar to everyone. He was a lobbyist and a stockbroker, a racegoer and an expert poker player. He was also a philanthropist, a man who was described as the "soul of honor." Yet his obituary in the *New York Times* opened with a reference to the Rickey, the cocktail that was created at Shoemaker's in Washington, D.C. and bears his name. That's what is known as getting your priorities right!

preparation In advance: Chill the glass.

mixing Fill the glass with ice. Add the gin and lime juice and stir. Top up with club soda.

garnish Garnish with lime wedges.

Like this? Try this
▸ **Gimlet,** *page 49*

Whiskey Rickey

Use a blended whiskey for this, and be generous with the fresh lime juice—they work really well together. And be warned—this is one of those cocktails that could start to get confusing after you've had a few. You'll feel very silly if you hear yourself saying: "Anyone for another Risky Whiskey?"

preparation In advance: Chill the glass.

mixing Fill the glass with ice. Add the whiskey and lime juice and stir. Top up with club soda.

garnish Garnish with lime wedges.

mixing ingredients
▶ 3 parts (1½ fl oz/45 ml) blended whiskey
▶ 2 parts (1 fl oz/30 ml) freshly squeezed lime juice
▶ club soda, to top up

you will also need
▶ Ice cubes
▶ Lime wedges

bar tools
▶ Lowball glass
▶ Bar spoon

Cost ￥￥
Degree of difficulty 🍋

City Rickey

As you might expect for a cocktail with "City" in the name, this is a very chic Rickey. It says that you have traditional values but you're not stuck in the past. You're firmly grounded but not afraid to take risks. You're an individual but you respect others. Are you buying any of this? It just tastes good, people!

preparation In advance: Chill the glass.

mixing Fill the glass with ice. Add the gin, orange liqueur, lime juice, and cranberry juice and stir. Top up with club soda.

garnish Garnish with orange slices.

mixing ingredients
▶ 3 parts (1½ fl oz/45 ml) gin
▶ 2 parts (1 fl oz/30 ml) orange liqueur
▶ 1 part (½ fl oz/15 ml) freshly squeezed lime juice
▶ 4 parts (2 fl oz/60 ml) cranberry juice
▶ 4 parts (2 fl oz/60 ml) club soda

you will also need
▶ Ice cubes
▶ Orange slices

bar tools
▶ Highball glass
▶ Bar spoon

Cost ￥￥
Degree of difficulty 🍋

Long Island Iced Tea

This cocktail is every bit as elegant as its name suggests, and although it looks—and even tastes—like iced tea, none of its long list of ingredients has even the remotest connection with that innocent beverage. This is a brew that really packs a punch. Robert "Rosebud" Butt, bartender at the Oak Beach Inn, Hampton Bays, Long Island, New York, is credited as the inventor of the drink, back in 1976, though inevitably there are plenty of other stories about its origins. A rather entertaining version suggests that it was thrown together (literally, from the entire contents of the bar cabinet) by bored Long Island housewives...

mixing ingredients
▶ 1 part (½ fl oz/15 ml) gin
▶ 1 part (½ fl oz/15 ml) tequila
▶ 1 part (½ fl oz/15 ml) triple sec
▶ 1 part (½ fl oz/15 ml) vodka
▶ 1 part (½ fl oz/15 ml) white rum
▶ 1½ parts (¾ oz/22 ml) sweet and sour mix
▶ cola, to top up

you will also need
▶ Ice cubes
▶ Cucumber curl
▶ Cocktail pick

bar tools
▶ Highball glass
▶ Mixing glass
▶ Bar spoon
▶ Cocktail shaker
▶ Strainer

Cost ▆▆▆
Degree of difficulty

preparation In advance: Chill the glass.

mixing Pour all the ingredients except the cola into the mixing glass and stir. Pour over ice in the cocktail shaker and shake once. Strain over ice in the highball glass and top up with cola.

garnish Garnish with a cucumber curl on a cocktail pick.

Like this? Try this
▶ **Blue Lagoon,** *page 97*

Singapore Sling

mixing ingredients
▶ 2 parts (1 fl oz/30 ml) gin
▶ 1 part (½ fl oz/15 ml) cherry brandy
▶ ½ part (1/4 fl oz/7.5 ml) Cointreau®
▶ ½ part (1/4 fl oz/7.5 ml) Bénédictine®
▶ 8 parts (4 fl oz/120 ml) pineapple juice
▶ 1 part (½ fl oz/15 ml) lime juice
▶ 2 teaspoons grenadine
▶ 1 dash Angostura® bitters

you will also need
▶ Ice cubes
▶ Lime wedges

bar tools
(for all three versions)
▶ Hurricane or highball glass
▶ Cocktail shaker
▶ Strainer

Cost ♈♈♈
Degree of difficulty

Singapore's Raffles Hotel (named for the city's founder, Sir Stamford Raffles) is famous for many things, not least for simply being itself—sumptuous, elegant, luxurious. Over the last century or so, its magnificent suites have welcomed endless celebs, from Jean Harlow to Rudy Giuliani. Raffles has its own march, composed in 1915 by A. Dietz; and it has its own cocktails, the Million Dollar and the Singapore Sling, created by bartender Ngiam Tong Boon a few years earlier. If you haven't scheduled a visit to Raffles this year, at least try this cocktail …

preparation In advance: Chill the glass.

mixing Shake the ingredients briskly with ice. Strain over ice in the glass.

garnish Garnish with lime wedges.

Like this? Try this
▶ **Rose,** page 165

Thai Sling

Thai bartenders have responded to the Singapore Sling with a pretty good version of their own. What makes it "Thai"? It's the palm sugar, sold in various forms including curious little cone shapes that you have to shave or shred. You can use brown sugar instead, but your Thai Sling will be a little less—*Thai*.

preparation In advance: Chill the glass.

mixing Shake all the ingredients except the pineapple juice briskly with ice. Strain over ice in the glass and top up with pineapple juice.

garnish Garnish with a pineapple wedge.

mixing ingredients
▶ 2 parts (1 fl oz/30 ml) whiskey
▶ 1 part (½ fl oz/15 ml) cherry brandy
▶ 1 part (½ fl oz/15 ml) triple sec
▶ 1 part (½ fl oz/15 ml) freshly squeezed lime juice
▶ 1 teaspoon palm sugar (or brown sugar)
▶ 1 dash Angostura® bitters
▶ Fresh pineapple juice, to top up

you will also need
▶ Ice cubes
▶ Pineapple wedge

Cost Y Y Y
Degree of difficulty 🍊🍊

Gin Sling

The Gin Sling is a much simpler version of the original Singapore Sling. You only need gin and sweet vermouth in your bar cabinet for this one, but you still get an appetizing balance of sweet/sour flavors. It's also—let's face it—rather less expensive to make. Perhaps it should be renamed the "Weekday Sling!"

preparation In advance: Chill the glass.

mixing Shake all the ingredients except the club soda briskly with ice. Strain over ice in the glass and top up with club soda.

garnish Garnish with a twist of lemon zest.

mixing ingredients
▶ 3 parts (1½ fl oz/45 ml) gin
▶ 2 parts (1 fl oz/30 ml) sweet vermouth
▶ 1½ parts (¾ fl oz/22.5 ml) freshly squeezed lemon juice
▶ 2 parts (1 fl oz/30 ml) sugar syrup
▶ 1 dash Angostura® bitters
▶ Club soda, to top up

you will also need
▶ Ice cubes
▶ Twist of lemon zest

Cost Y Y
Degree of difficulty 🍊🍊

mixing ingredients
▸ 4 parts (2 fl oz/60 ml) bourbon whiskey
▸ 2 parts (1 fl oz/30 ml) freshly squeezed lemon juice
▸ 1 teaspoon sugar
▸ club soda, to top up

you will also need
▸ Ice cubes
▸ Orange slices

bar tools
▸ Highball glass
▸ Bar spoon

Cost
Degree of difficulty

John Collins

Nothing stirs up controversy quite like the origins of a cocktail and the Collins is no exception. In 1891, a British physician claimed that the Tom Collins was named after a song called "John Collins," which turned out in fact to be Jim, not John. So should the bourbon-based John Collins really be called a Jim Collins?

preparation In advance: Chill the glass.

mixing Fill the glass with ice. Add the bourbon, lemon juice, and sugar and stir. Top up with club soda.

garnish Garnish with orange slices.

mixing ingredients
▸ 4 parts (2 fl oz/60 ml) vodka or lime vodka
▸ 2 parts (1 fl oz/30 ml) freshly squeezed lemon juice
▸ 1 teaspoon sugar
▸ club soda, to top up

you will also need
▸ Ice cubes
▸ Lemon or lime slices

bar tools
▸ Highball glass
▸ Bar spoon

Cost
Degree of difficulty

Vodka Collins

This is a refreshing variation on the Tom Collins cocktail. It's delicious with standard vodka, but you might try ringing the changes with a lime-flavored vodka. Vodka Collins, incidentally, is also the name of a popular but highly controversial 1970s Japanese-American glam-rock band. Wonder what their favorite cocktail was?

preparation In advance: Chill the glass.

mixing Fill the glass with ice. Add the vodka, lemon juice, and sugar and stir. Top up with club soda.

garnish Garnish with lemon or lime slices.

Tom Collins

A Tom Collins is all the more enjoyable when you know the story of the Great Tom Collins Hoax. The hoax began in the US in 1874, and was played like this: A person would stop an acquaintance in the street and ask, "Have you seen Tom Collins?" "I don't know any Tom Collins," the hapless acquaintance would reply. "Oh, but he knows you—he's been spreading gossip about you. He's in that bar around the corner." Whereupon the irate acquaintance would set off in hot pursuit of the imaginary Collins...

preparation In advance: Chill the glass.

mixing Fill the glass with ice. Add the gin, lemon juice, and sugar and stir. Top up with club soda.

garnish Garnish with lemon slices.

Like this? Try this
▶ **Gin Rickey,** *page 100*

mixing ingredients
▶ 4 parts (2 fl oz/60 ml) gin
▶ 2 parts (1 fl oz/30 ml) freshly squeezed lemon juice
▶ 1 teaspoon sugar
▶ club soda, to top up

you will also need
▶ Ice cubes
▶ Lemon slices

bar tools
▶ Highball glass
▶ Bar spoon

Cost ♟♟
Degree of difficulty

Caipirinha

The Caipirinha ("kai-pur-een-yah") is
the national cocktail of Brazil, and was once a closely
guarded concoction—but now the secret's out, and
it's proved so popular it's even made it onto the
International Bartenders' Association official list.
The key ingredient of a caipirinha (from a Portuguese
word, roughly translated meaning "yokel") is cachaça,
a Brazilian-style rum made from fermented sugarcane
juice. And here's the best bit—when making a caipirinha,
you get to muddle with a muddler and after you've
sampled a couple you might well be muddled when
you're muddling with the muddler…

preparation In advance: Chill the glass.

mixing Cut the limes into wedges, place them in the glass
with the sugar, and muddle vigorously. Fill the glass with
crushed ice, add the cachaça, and stir briskly. Garnish with
lemon and lime zest and a lemon slice. Keep stirring
as you sip, to ensure the sugar stays well mixed.

mixing ingredients
▸ 2 small, juicy limes
▸ 2 teaspoons superfine
sugar
▸ 4 parts (2 fl oz/60 ml)
cachaça

you will also need
▸ Crushed ice
▸ Lemon and lime zest
▸ Lemon slice

bar tools
▸ Highball glass
▸ Muddler or wooden spoon
▸ Bar spoon

Cost ΥΥ
Degree of
difficulty ✹✹

Like this? Try this
▸ **Daiquiri,** *page 51*

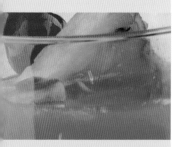

Hurricane

One Pat O'Brien, who kept a tavern in the French Quarter of New Orleans during the 1940s, was persuaded by an artful liquor salesman to acquire a stock of more bottles of rum than he could handle. Desperate to dispose of it, he mixed together the white and dark rum with lime juice and passion-fruit syrup, poured it into glasses shaped like hurricane lamps, and gave it away. The concoction he threw together so hastily proved to be a lasting success—in fact, it's as popular as ever at Pat O'Brien's bar, where the motto is: "Have fun!" This is one hurricane with which you'll absolutely love a close encounter!

mixing ingredients
▶ 2 parts (1 fl oz/30 ml) white rum
▶ 2 parts (1 fl oz/30 ml) gold or dark rum
▶ 4 parts (2 fl oz/60 ml) passion-fruit syrup
▶ 2 parts (1 fl oz/30 ml) freshly squeezed lime juice
▶ 1 part (½ fl oz/15 ml) grenadine

you will also need
▶ Ice cubes
▶ Pineapple wedges
▶ Maraschino cherry
▶ Cocktail umbrella

bar tools
▶ Hurricane or highball glass
▶ Cocktail shaker
▶ Strainer

Cost ΥΥ
Degree of difficulty

preparation In advance: Chill the glass.

mixing Shake the ingredients briskly with ice. Strain over ice cubes in the glass.

garnish Garnish with pineapple wedges, a maraschino cherry, and a cocktail umbrella.

Like this? Try this
▶ **Babar,** *page 120*

Americano

In the 1940s, Gaspare Campari, a precocious 14-year-old, started work in a Turin bar washing dishes, and within a year was apprentice to the master drink maker. In 1860 he opened his own café in Milan, where he created the secret blend of herbs, spices, bark, and fruit peels that bear his name. He mixed Campari® bitters with sweet vermouth and called the cocktail a Milano-Torino to reflect the origins of the ingredients, but it was renamed the Americano during Prohibition in honor of some *very* appreciative American visitors.

mixing ingredients
▶ 2 parts (1 fl oz/30 ml) Campari®
▶ 2 parts (1 fl oz/30 ml) sweet vermouth
▶ 2 parts (1 fl oz/30 ml) club soda

you will also need
▶ Ice cubes
▶ Orange slices

bar tools
▶ Highball glass
▶ Bar spoon

Cost 🍸🍸
Degree of difficulty 🍊

preparation In advance: Chill the glass.

mixing Fill the glass with ice. Pour in the Campari® and sweet vermouth, stir once, and add the soda.

garnish Garnish with orange slices.

Like this? Try this
▶ **Eden,** *page 41*

Negroni

General Pascal Olivier Count de Negroni was born in a castle—and not many people can claim that. He had a long and distinguished career in the French Army for which he was awarded several honors. Not many people can claim that, either. And he adored this cocktail. At least we can share that bit...

preparation In advance: Chill the glass.

mixing Pour the ingredients over ice in the glass and stir.

garnish Garnish with a twist of orange zest.

mixing ingredients
▸ 2 parts (1 fl oz/30 ml) gin
▸ 2 parts (1 fl oz/30 ml) Campari®
▸ 2 parts (1 fl oz/30 ml) sweet vermouth

you will also need
▸ Ice cubes
▸ Twist of orange zest

bar tools
▸ Lowball glass
▸ Bar spoon

Cost ▼▼▼
Degree of difficulty 🍊

Campari Lady

Don't let the name fool you: there's nothing demure about this cocktail—it's got plenty of attitude! On the other hand, ladies, you could take a sip, reach for your lace handkerchief, let it drift to your daintily shod feet, flutter your eyelashes at a passing knight in shining armor... come on, you never know!

preparation In advance: Chill the glass.

mixing Shake the ingredients briskly with ice. Strain over ice in the glass.

garnish Garnish with a twist of ruby red grapefruit zest.

mixing ingredients
▸ 3 parts (1½ fl oz/45 ml) Campari®
▸ 2 parts (1 fl oz/30 ml) gin
▸ 8 parts (4 fl oz/120 ml) freshly squeezed ruby grapefruit juice
▸ 2 parts (1 fl oz/30 ml) tonic water

you will also need
▸ Ice cubes
▸ Twist of ruby red grapefruit zest

bar tools
▸ Highball glass
▸ Cocktail shaker
▸ Strainer

Cost ▼▼
Degree of difficulty

Like this? Try this
▸ **Caipirinha,**
page 109

Mojito

It's not just the ice that makes the Mojito one of the coolest cocktails around! Its popularity is impressive for a drink that's been around for several hundred years. Its origins lie in the 16th century, when the Draque, a concoction of *aquardiente* (a crude form of rum), sugar, lime, and mint, was imbibed for medicinal purposes—yes, we've all heard *that* excuse... In the mid-1800s rum replaced the *aquardiente* and the name changed to Mojito, from the African word *mojo*, meaning "to place a little spell." As all Mojito fans know, it certainly works magic!

preparation In advance: Chill the glass.

mixing Muddle the mint leaves with the sugar and lime juice in the glass until the mint aroma is released. Add ice cubes, then pour over the rum and top up with the soda.

garnish Garnish with lime wedges and a sprig of mint.

mixing ingredients
▸ 4 fresh mint leaves
▸ 2 teaspoons sugar
▸ 2 parts (1 fl oz/30 ml) freshly squeezed lime juice
▸ 4 parts (2 fl oz/60 ml) white rum
▸ 4 parts (2 fl oz/60 ml) club soda

you will also need
▸ Ice cubes
▸ Lime wedges
▸ Fresh mint sprigs

bar tools
▸ Highball glass
▸ Muddler

Cost ♈♈
Degree of difficulty

Cuba Libre

According to a charming but chronologically dubious legend, a group of US soldiers were spending off-duty time in a bar in Old Havana, Cuba at the end of the Spanish-American War when a captain came in, ordered a gold rum and cola on ice with a wedge of lime, and drank it with obvious pleasure. The soldiers, intrigued, ordered the same and soon everyone was in such a mellow mood that the captain proposed a toast to the newly liberated island: "Por Cuba Libre!" As for that discrepancy over dates, cola only appeared in Cuba some time *after* the alleged toast was made...

mixing ingredients
- 2 parts (1 fl oz/30 ml) gold or white rum
- 2 parts (1 fl oz/30 ml) cola
- 1½ teaspoons freshly squeezed lime or lemon juice
- cola, to top up

you will also need
- Ice cubes
- Lime or lemon slice
- Fresh mint (optional)

bar tools
- Highball glass
- Cocktail shaker
- Bar spoon

Cost ΥΥ
Degree of difficulty ✹✹

preparation In advance: Chill the glass.

mixing Shake the measured ingredients briskly with ice. Strain over ice cubes in the glass, top up with cola—a little at a time—to taste, and stir lightly.

garnish Garnish with a lime or lemon slice and a sprig of fresh mint, if you wish.

Like this? Try this
▶ **Long Island Iced Tea,** *page 102*

Harvey Wallbanger

The star of the best story attached to this curiously named 1970s cocktail is a Californian surfer called Harvey. After losing a major surfing contest, Harvey headed to a bar owned by world champion mixologist Donato "Duke" Antone and drowned his sorrows in rather more Screwdrivers than were strictly necessary, each spiked with a shot of Galliano®. His eventual exit from the bar involved much stumbling into walls and furniture, and from that day both he and his tipple were known as—yes, you've got it.

mixing ingredients
▶ 2 parts (1 fl oz/30 ml) vodka
▶ 6 parts (3 fl oz/90 ml) freshly squeezed orange juice
▶ 1 part (½ fl oz/15 ml) Galliano®

you will also need
▶ Ice cubes
▶ Orange slice
▶ Maraschino cherry

bar tools
▶ Highball glass
▶ Cocktail shaker
▶ Strainer

Cost 🍸🍸
Degree of difficulty 🍊🍊

preparation In advance: Chill the glass.

mixing Shake the vodka and orange juice briskly with ice. Strain over ice in the glass and float the Galliano® on top.

garnish Garnish with an orange slice and a maraschino cherry.

Like this? Try this
▶ **Screwdriver,** *page 147*

Mint Julep

Some things in life just go together, and some traditions simply must be observed. For example, the Wimbledon Tennis Championships go hand-in-hand with strawberries and cream; the Venice Carnival always culminates in a feast of *frittolle*; and to stage the Kentucky Derby without Mint Julep would be nothing short of sacrilege. It's been the custom for around a hundred years, and whether you're celebrating a big win or drowning your sorrows, be really chic and drink your julep from a silver or pewter cup—hold it by the rims, to avoid melting the frost.

preparation In advance: Chill the julep cup or highball glass. Fill with ice just before mixing.

mixing Muddle the mint leaves and sugar thoroughly in the mixing glass. Add the bourbon, stir, and strain over the ice in the julep cup or highball glass.

garnish Garnish with a sprig of fresh mint.

mixing ingredients
▸ 12 fresh mint leaves
▸ 4 teaspoons superfine sugar
▸ 5 parts (2½ fl oz/75 ml) bourbon whiskey

you will also need
▸ Crushed ice
▸ Fresh mint sprig

bar tools
▸ Julep cup
(or highball glass)
▸ Mixing glass
▸ Muddler
▸ Bar spoon

Cost ♟♟
Degree of difficulty

Like this? Try this
▸ **Mojito,** *page 115*

Babar

mixing ingredients
▸ 3 parts (1½ fl oz/45 ml) vodka
▸ 1 part (½ fl oz/15 ml) Passoã®
▸ 3 parts (1½ fl oz/45 ml) guanabana juice
▸ 2 parts (1 fl oz/30 ml) cranberry juice
▸ lemon-lime flavor soda, to top up

you will also need
▸ Ice cubes
▸ Fresh mint sprig

bar tools
▸ Highball glass
▸ Bar spoon

Cost 🍸🍸
Degree of difficulty ◉

Like this? Try this
▸ **Hurricane,**
page 110

Here's a cocktail with a couple of unusual ingredients. The first is Passoã®, a passion-fruit liqueur that instantly conjures up visions of sunshine and fiestas. It comes in an intriguing black bottle, which is fun—if you like a challenge, such as guessing how much is left! The second is guanabana juice—no, not a made-up name, just the Spanish word for the curiously spiny soursop, a fruit that can't quite make up its mind what to taste like. Think mango, pineapple, strawberry, maybe a little vanilla, and you're getting close.

preparation In advance: Chill the glass.

mixing Pour the vodka, Passoã®, guanabana juice, and cranberry juice over ice in the glass. Stir, then top up with lemon-lime flavor soda.

garnish Garnish with a sprig of fresh mint.

Woo Woo

There are many different recipes for this cocktail, and the one you choose will determine the tone in which you exclaim "Woo Woo!" after taking your first sip. For example, if you use equal parts of vodka and peach schnapps, your slightly schocked (sorry, shocked) "Woo Woo" will be followed by "Too sweet!" If, as some suggest, you use more peach schnapps than vodka, you'll cry "Woo Woo! Too fruity!" But try this recipe and you're guaranteed to say, "Woo Woo! Just perfect!"

mixing ingredients
▶ 4 parts (2 fl oz/60 ml) vodka
▶ 1 part (½ fl oz/15 ml) peach schnapps
▶ 8 parts (4 fl oz/120 ml) cranberry juice

you will also need
▶ Ice cubes

bar tools
▶ Highball glass
▶ Cocktail shaker
▶ Strainer

Cost ¥¥
Degree of difficulty

preparation In advance: Chill the glass.

mixing Shake the ingredients briskly with ice. Strain over ice in the glass.

Like this? Try this
▶ **Fire Starter,** *page 185*

Like this? Try this
▶ **Lemonade,**
page 136

Chili Queen

This is carrot juice 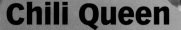 with attitude, named after the Mexican "chili queens" who, in the late 19th and early 20th centuries, sold dishes of fiery chili con carne throughout the night from colorful, brightly lit wagons on the Military, Haymarket, and Alamo Plazas in San Antonio, Texas. The tradition was brought to an abrupt end in 1937 by the health department, but the chili queens live on in memory, gastronomy—and cocktails.

mixing ingredients
▶ 2 carrots
▶ ½ small pineapple
▶ ½ small red chili
▶ 1 lime, freshly squeezed

you will also need
▶ Ice cubes
▶ 1 tablespoon cilantro leaves, chopped
▶ Fresh cilantro or flat-leaf parsley sprig

bar tools
▶ Highball glass
▶ Juice extractor

Cost 🍸
Degree of difficulty

preparation In advance: Chill the glass. Juice the carrots, pineapple, and chili in a juice extractor.

mixing Stir the carrot, pineapple, and chili juice together, then stir in the lime juice. Pour over ice in the glass.

garnish Sprinkle with chopped cilantro and garnish with a sprig of fresh cilantro or flat-leaf parsley.

Runner's Mark

This can be a morning-after life-saver or just a great way to start the day, depending on the circumstances. It's oozing with vitamin C, which if you've over-imbibed will stimulate your liver to metabolize the alcohol. You can use a ready-made vegetable juice, or make your own (assuming, of course, that you can stand the noise of the juice extractor). Add the lemon juice and wake-up sauces, knock it back, and within moments you'll be on your marks and ready to go, go, GO!

Like this? Try this
▸ **Bloody Mary,** *page 150*

mixing ingredients
▸ 8 parts (4 fl oz/120 ml) vegetable juice
▸ 2 drops lemon juice
▸ 2 drops Tabasco® sauce
▸ 1 dash Worcestershire® sauce

you will also need
▸ Ice cubes
▸ Celery stalk with leaves

bar tools
▸ Lowball glass
▸ Bar spoon

preparation In advance: Chill the glass.

mixing Pour the ingredients over ice in the glass and stir.

garnish Garnish with a leafy celery stalk.

Cost Y
Degree of difficulty ◉

5

Fresh and fruity

Pimm's® Cup

Pimm's® is traditionally a must-have at events throughout the English high society "season," such as the Wimbledon Lawn Tennis Championships and Henley Royal Regatta. In 1823 James Pimm, the owner of a City of London oyster bar, first served the original drink—a blend of gin and herbs—to his customers as a digestive aid. It obviously worked wonders—by the middle of the century Mr. Pimm had refined his recipe and gone into large-scale production. The magic concoction was served in a tankard, the "No. 1 Cup."

SERVES 10
mixing ingredients
▶ 2 cups (1 pint/500 ml) Pimm's No. 1®
▶ 6 cups (3 pints/1.5 liters) lemonade
▶ 1 orange, sliced
▶ 1 lemon, sliced
▶ ½ cucumber, sliced
▶ fresh mint sprigs

you will also need
▶ Ice cubes
▶ Fresh orange, sliced
▶ Fresh mint sprigs

bar tools
▶ Pitcher
▶ Highball glasses
▶ Cocktail stirrer

Cost
Degree of difficulty ✦

preparation In advance: Chill the pitcher and glasses.

mixing Pour the Pimm's No. 1® and the lemonade over ice cubes in the chilled pitcher, add the remaining ingredients, and stir to combine. Serve in the chilled glasses.

garnish Garnish each serving with an orange slice and a sprig of fresh mint.

Like this? Try this
▶ **Mojito,** *page 115*

mixing ingredients
▸ 2 parts (1 fl oz/30 ml) vodka
▸ 2 parts (1 fl oz/30 ml) apricot brandy
▸ 2 parts (1 fl oz/30 ml) banana liqueur
▸ 1 part (½ fl oz/15 ml) freshly squeezed lime juice
▸ ¼ small banana, thinly sliced
▸ club soda or carbonated water, to top up

you will also need
▸ Ice cubes
▸ Slice of banana
▸ Strip of banana peel
▸ Fresh mint sprig

bar tools
▸ Stemmed tulip glass
▸ Cocktail shaker
▸ Strainer

Cost ♈♈♈
Degree of difficulty ◉◉

Like this? Try this
▸ **Banana Colada,**
page 144

Banana Punch

The word "punch" is thought to derive from the Sanskrit word *pañca*, meaning five. That's the number of ingredients that traditionally go into a punch—and they can be any five you like. Banana Punch sounds innocent enough to serve at your kid's birthday party, but this potent combo is for the grown-ups only—for everyone else, blend bananas with sugar syrup or honey and mix with lemonade, orange juice, and ginger ale. Quick count—yes, that's five!

preparation In advance: Chill the glass.

mixing Shake the vodka, apricot brandy, banana liqueur, and lime juice briskly with ice. Strain into the glass over the banana slices and ice, and top up with soda or carbonated water.

garnish Garnish with the banana slice, the strip of banana peel, and a sprig of fresh mint.

Planter's Punch

Planter's Punch, traditionally served as a "welcome" drink in the Caribbean, made its first appearance in print in *The New York Times* in 1908, as the subject of a poem, of all things! The poet was obviously pretty confident of his recipe—he ended his poem with words born of experience: "I know whereof I speak."

preparation In advance: Chill the glass.

mixing Shake the ingredients briskly with ice. Strain over ice into the glass.

garnish Garnish with the orange slice and a sprinkling of freshly ground nutmeg and cinnamon.

mixing ingredients
- 4 parts (2 fl oz/60 ml) dark rum
- 4 parts (2 fl oz/60 ml) fresh pineapple juice
- 4 parts (2 fl oz/60 ml) freshly squeezed orange juice
- 1 part (½ fl oz/15 ml) freshly squeezed lime juice
- pinch each ground nutmeg and cinnamon

you will also need
- Ice cubes
- Orange slice
- Freshly grated nutmeg

bar tools
- Highball glass
- Cocktail shaker
- Strainer

Cost ▼▼
Degree of difficulty ●●

Ti Punch

"Ti" is not a mysterious cocktail ingredient, but a derivation from the French word for little, *petit*. Now, it might *mean* an affectionate little punch, but this drink packs quite a big punch ... And there *is* an ingredient that you might not know—*rhum agricole*, made from freshly squeezed sugar cane juice.

preparation In advance: Chill the glass.

mixing Squeeze the juice from the lime into the glass and add the syrup. Add the rum and stir well, then add the ice cubes and stir again.

mixing ingredients
- ½ fresh lime
- 1 part (½ fl oz/15 ml) sugar cane syrup
- 4 parts (2 fl oz/60 ml) white *rhum agricole*

you will also need
- Ice cubes

bar tools
- Lowball glass
- Bar spoon

Cost ▼▼
Degree of difficulty

Appletini

Appletini is the wholesome name of a cocktail that's considerably more lethal than it sounds. It was invented in the 1970s by Barry Lovern, a hotel bartender in County Galway, Ireland. The triple sec in Lovern's original recipe is replaced here with melon liqueur to give it a vibrant green color, reminiscent of—apples! If you want to take the whole thing down a notch, you can use a fresh, sharp apple juice instead of the schnapps.

mixing ingredients
▸ 3 parts (1½ fl oz/45 ml) vodka
▸ 1 part (½ fl oz/15 ml) apple schnapps
▸ 1 part (½ fl oz/15 ml) melon liqueur

you will also need
▸ Ice cubes
▸ Apple peel twist

bar tools
▸ Stemmed cocktail glass
▸ Cocktail shaker
▸ Strainer

Cost ▼▼▼
Degree of difficulty 🍊🍊

preparation In advance: Chill the glass.

mixing Shake the ingredients briskly with ice. Strain into the glass.

garnish Garnish with an apple peel twist.

Like this? Try this
▸ **Garden of Eden,**
page 40

Frozen Margaritas

Yes, cocktail drinkers, we're going to reconnect with our inner child—the one that likes to drink frozen slush, get an ice-cream headache, and run round screaming noisily in an arm-flapping frenzy while the effect wears off. The real children, meanwhile, can be very grown-up and stand to one side, watching more in sorrow than in anger... These frozen Margaritas look sensational, taste fabulous, and are really good fun—just make sure everyone knows they're strictly for the over-21s!

preparation In advance: Chill the glass. Just before serving, scatter some salt on a paper towel (or use granulated sugar for the strawberry flavor). Rub the lime wedge around the rim of the glass, then dip the rim into the salt or sugar.

mixing Blend the ingredients briefly to combine. Decant into the glass and serve immediately.

Garnish Garnish with a lime slice.

mixing ingredients
▸ 2 parts (1 fl oz/30 ml) tequila (100 percent agave)
▸ 1 part (½ fl oz/15 ml) triple sec
▸ 1 part (½ fl oz/15 ml) freshly squeezed orange, lemon, or lime juice or frozen strawberry purée
▸ ½ cup crushed ice

you will also need
▸ Coarse salt or granulated sugar
▸ Lime wedge
▸ Lime slice

bar tools
▸ Margarita glass
▸ Blender

Cost 🍸🍸
Degree of difficulty ✹

Like this? Try this
▸ **Tequila Canyon,** *page 140*

Pomegranate Mojito

The pomegranate is a fascinating fruit: beautiful in appearance (if a little strange), and if you did no more than arrange a few in a decorative dish, you'd already feel rather pleased with your purchase. Cut into one, however, and you find the real treasure—a whole casket of little seeds looking just like tiny rubies. If you're an extremely patient person, you can release these from their tenacious casing and make your own pomegranate juice to go in this cocktail. Everyone else, buy it in a carton...

preparation In advance: Chill the glass.

mixing Muddle the mint leaves with the sugar and lime juice in the mixing glass. Add ice cubes, then stir in the rum and pomegranate juice. Strain over ice in the lowball glass and top up with soda.

garnish Garnish with a lemon zest twist or with a lime slice and a sprig of mint.

Like this? Try this
▸ **Dusk in Eden,** *page 40*

mixing ingredients
▸ 5 fresh mint leaves
▸ 2 teaspoons sugar
▸ 1 part (½ fl oz/15 ml) freshly squeezed lime juice
▸ 3 parts (1½ fl oz/45 ml) white rum
▸ 2 parts (1 fl oz/30 ml) pomegranate juice
▸ club soda, to top up

you will also need
▸ Ice cubes
▸ Lemon zest twist or lime slice
▸ Fresh mint sprig

bar tools
▸ Lowball glass
▸ Mixing glass
▸ Muddler
▸ Bar spoon
▸ Strainer

Cost ￥￥
Degree of difficulty ✺✺

Jamaican Sunset

There is much speculation over the origin of the word "rum." One explanation is that it's short for "rumbullion," an expressive but now sadly obsolete word meaning "uproar;" another is that it's taken from the gypsy word *rum*, meaning "potent." We might never know, but one thing's for sure—a heady combination of spiced rum and dark rum with orange and pineapple looks just like a glowing Jamaican sunset.

mixing ingredients
- 2 parts + ½ tablespoon (1¼ fl oz/37.5 ml) spiced rum
- 1 part (½ fl oz/15 ml) dark rum
- 3 parts (1½ fl oz/45 ml) fresh pineapple juice
- 3 parts (1½ fl oz/45 ml) freshly squeezed orange juice
- 2 parts (1 fl oz/30 ml) sweet and sour mix

you will also need
- Ice cubes
- Pineapple wedge
- Maraschino cherry
- Wooden toothpick

bar tools
- Hurricane or highball glass
- Cocktail shaker
- Strainer

Cost
Degree of difficulty

preparation In advance: Chill the glass.

mixing Shake the ingredients briskly with ice. Strain over ice cubes in the glass.

garnish Garnish with a pineapple wedge and fix a maraschino cherry to the pineapple using a wooden toothpick.

Like this? Try this

▶ **Pineapple Mai Tai,** *page 95*

Operation Recoverer

We all know how important it is to eat plenty of fruit after surgery—that's why it's the classic gift to offer a convalescent. Lots of vitamin C to speed up the healing and vibrant color to cheer the patient, who might be feeling a little disoriented—and certainly will be if he or she drinks this cocktail. So in spite of its name and all the delicious fruit flavors, it's probably best to save the Operation Recoverer for occasions when everyone is in good health!

preparation In advance: Chill the glass.

mixing Shake the ingredients briskly with ice. Strain over ice in the glass.

garnish Garnish with a lime slice, a maraschino cherry, and a sprig of fresh mint.

Like this? Try this
▶ **Fireworks,** *page 184*

mixing ingredients
▶ 2 parts (1 fl oz/30 ml) lemon vodka
▶ 2 parts (1 fl oz/30 ml) peach schnapps
▶ 4 parts (2 fl oz/60 ml) freshly squeezed tangerine juice
▶ 1 teaspoon grenadine

you will also need
▶ Ice cubes
▶ Lime slice
▶ Maraschino cherry
▶ Fresh mint sprig

bar tools
▶ Lowball glass
▶ Cocktail shaker
▶ Strainer

Cost ￥￥
Degree of difficulty

Lemonade

This one's for drivers and non-drinkers—cool, refreshing, homemade lemonade. It's just delicious, and so evocative of long summer days spent outdoors. Traditionally, lemonade is made from uncarbonated water, but carbonated water lends a festive sparkle. To turn your lemonade an irresistible shade of pink, add a dash of grenadine or cranberry juice. This will certainly taste better than the original pink lemonade, if claims are true that one Pete Conklin invented it by chance in 1857 when he made lemonade from water colored by a circus rider's red tights...

SERVES 6

mixing ingredients
▶ ¾–1 cup (6–8 oz/175–225 g) sugar, to taste
▶ 4 cups (2 pints/1 liter) spring water
▶ freshly squeezed juice of 4 lemons

you will also need
▶ Ice cubes
▶ Fresh lemon, sliced

bar tools
▶ Pitcher
▶ Highball glasses
▶ Bar spoon

Cost 🍸
Degree of difficulty 🍋

preparation In advance: Chill a pitcher and the glasses. Heat the sugar with 1 cup (8 fl oz/250 ml) of the water to dissolve the sugar. Cool, then chill in the refrigerator.

mixing Pour the chilled sugar syrup over ice cubes in the chilled pitcher with the remaining water and the lemon juice, and stir to combine.

garnish Add the lemon slices to the pitcher before serving.

Like this?
Try this
▶ **Pimm's Cup,**
page 126

Carambola Cocktail

When Mother Nature invented the carambola, she must have had cocktails in mind: a thin slice of this crisp, juicy, tropical fruit makes the most attractive, star-shaped garnish! There are several varieties—you'll find that the greener ones usually taste sweeter than the yellow. You can blend the fruit unpeeled, but remember to trim off the dark green edges if you want to avoid a bitter flavor that no amount of cherry brandy will ever disguise...

mixing ingredients
▸ 4 parts (2 fl oz/60 ml) fresh pineapple juice
▸ 2 parts (1 fl oz/30 ml) freshly squeezed orange juice
▸ ½ carambola fruit, trimmed
▸ 4 parts (2 fl oz/60 ml) vodka
▸ 4 parts (2 fl oz/60 ml) cherry brandy

you will also need
▸ Ice cubes
▸ Carambola slice

bar tools
▸ Tulip or lowball glass
▸ Blender
▸ Cocktail shaker
▸ Strainer

Cost 🍸🍸
Degree of difficulty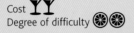

preparation In advance: Chill the glass. Blend the pineapple and orange juice with the carambola fruit.

mixing Shake the ingredients briskly with ice. Strain into the glass.

Garnish Garnish with a carambola slice.

Like this? Try this
▸ **Alien Sky,** *page 148*

Tropical Martini

This cocktail is really rather special—all the fresh, tropical fruitiness of a long, cool drink, but scaled down to the most elegant proportions. The combination of citrus juices add just a hint of delicate color to the gin, and once the grenadine comes to rest at the bottom of the glass, the Tropical Martini looks just heavenly. You know, it's surprising how *poetic* a cocktail can make one feel...

Like this? Try this
▶ **Island Breeze,** *page 99*

preparation
In advance: Chill the glass.

mixing
Shake all the ingredients except the grenadine briskly with ice. Strain into the glass and pour in the grenadine.

garnish
Garnish with citrus peel pinwheels.

mixing ingredients
▶ 6 parts (3 fl oz/90 ml) gin
▶ 1 part (½ fl oz/15 ml) freshly squeezed lemon juice
▶ 1 part (½ fl oz/15 ml) freshly squeezed orange juice
▶ 1 part (½ fl oz/15 ml) freshly squeezed grapefruit juice
▶ 2 teaspoons grenadine

you will also need
▶ Ice cubes
▶ Citrus peel pinwheels

bar tools
▶ Stemmed cocktail glass
▶ Cocktail shaker
▶ Strainer

Cost ¥¥
Degree of difficulty

Tequila Sunset

mixing ingredients
▶ 4 parts (2 fl oz/60 ml) tequila
▶ 8 parts (4 fl oz/120 ml) freshly squeezed orange juice
▶ 1 part (½ fl oz/15 ml) blackberry brandy or crème de mûre

you will also need
▶ Ice cubes
▶ Maraschino cherry

bar tools
▶ Highball glass
▶ Bar spoon

Cost
Degree of difficulty

It's a natural law of the universe that what goes up must come down, and that includes the sun. Use blackberry brandy instead of Sunrise grenadine and you have a Tequila Sunset, which tastes delicious even though it may give the impression that some rather alarming weather conditions are about to hit!

preparation In advance: Chill the glass.

mixing Fill the glass with ice. Add the tequila and orange juice and stir. Add the blackberry brandy and stir lightly.

garnish Garnish with a maraschino cherry.

Tequila Canyon

mixing ingredients
▶ 3 parts (1½ fl oz/45 ml) tequila
▶ 1 dash triple sec
▶ 8 parts (4 fl oz/120 ml) cranberry juice
▶ 1 part (½ fl oz/15 ml) fresh pineapple juice
▶ 1 part (½ fl oz/15 ml) freshly squeezed orange juice

you will also need
▶ Crushed ice
▶ Pineapple wedge and fresh mint sprig

bar tools
▶ Highball glass
▶ Bar spoon

Cost
Degree of difficulty

The Tequila Canyon is the cocktail equivalent of the Grand Canyon. This amazing sight (the canyon, not the cocktail) is believed to have been created by the Colorado River over a period of six million years. The cocktail, a sight almost—but not quite—as amazing, can be created by you in about six minutes.

preparation In advance: Chill the glass.

mixing Fill the glass with ice. Add the tequila, triple sec, and cranberry juice and stir lightly. Add the pineapple juice and orange juice without stirring.

garnish Garnish with a pineapple wedge and fresh mint sprig.

Tequila Sunrise

Gene Sulit, bartender for the Arizona Biltmore Hotel in Phoenix, invented the Tequila Sunrise in the late 1930s, but tequila is the only ingredient he'd recognize in today's version—grenadine replaces his crème de cassis "rising sun" and orange juice portrays a more authentic dawn sky than club soda. Although it's traditional to serve the Tequila Sunrise at Mexican Cinco de Mayo celebrations, held to commemorate their victory over the French at the Battle of Pueblo on May 5 1862, it's fine to drink it any day you like.

preparation In advance: Chill the glass.

mixing Fill the glass with ice. Add the tequila and orange juice and stir. Add the grenadine and allow it to sink to the bottom of the glass.

garnish Garnish with a maraschino cherry.

mixing ingredients
▸ 4 parts (2 fl oz/60 ml) tequila
▸ 8 parts (4 fl oz/120 ml) freshly squeezed orange juice
▸ 1 part (½ fl oz/15 ml) grenadine

you will also need
▸ Ice cubes
▸ Maraschino cherry

bar tools
▸ Highball glass
▸ Bar spoon

Cost ㆎㆎ
Degree of difficulty

Like this? Try this
▸ **Mediterranean Martini,** *page 175*

Like this? Try this
▶ **Bramble,** *page 59*

Raspberry Cosmopolitan

Raspberry-flavored vodka? Really? Yes, really! And not only is it absolutely delicious, but it also makes the already pink Cosmopolitan seem even *more* pink! You can, of course, drink it without filling the glass with fresh raspberries, but where's the fun in that? And why pass up the chance to play the raspberry version of the traditional Halloween game of apple bobbing? The rules are: No hands, and you must eat every single raspberry without spilling a drop of your Cosmo cocktail!

mixing ingredients
▶ 4 parts (2 fl oz/60 ml) raspberry vodka
▶ 1½ parts (¾ fl oz/22.5 ml) triple sec
▶ 2 parts (1 fl oz/30 ml) cranberry juice
▶ 1 part (½ fl oz/15 ml) freshly squeezed lime juice

you will also need
▶ Ice cubes
▶ Fresh raspberries

bar tools
▶ Stemmed cocktail glass
▶ Cocktail shaker
▶ Strainer

Cost ▸ Y Y
Degree of difficulty

preparation In advance: Chill the glass.

mixing Shake the ingredients briskly with ice. Strain into the glass.

garnish Garnish with raspberries.

Like this? Try this
▸ **Cosmopolitan,** *page 172*

Sea Breeze

The ingredients for a Sea Breeze include grapefruit juice, not often used in cocktails. Grapefruit flesh comes in a range of colors, and the pinker the flesh, the sweeter it is—bear this in mind if you want to avoid the "grapefruit gasp and grimace" that inevitably follows an encounter with a very pale-fleshed variety! In the 1995 film *French Kiss*, the heroine, Kate, orders this cocktail on a beach in Cannes, in the South of France—surely the perfect location to enjoy the Sea Breeze.

preparation In advance: Chill the glass.

mixing Fill the glass with ice. Add the ingredients one at a time and stir once, very gently.

garnish Garnish with a lime slice and a maraschino cherry.

mixing ingredients
▸ 8 parts (4 fl oz/120 ml) cranberry juice
▸ 2 parts (1 fl oz/30 ml) freshly squeezed pink grapefruit juice
▸ 3 parts (1½ fl oz/45 ml) vodka

you will also need
▸ Ice cubes
▸ Lime slice
▸ Maraschino cherry

bar tools
▸ Highball glass
▸ Bar spoon

Cost ⅄⅄
Degree of difficulty

mixing ingredients
▶ 3 parts (1½ fl oz/45 ml) white rum
▶ 1 part (½ fl oz/15 ml) strawberry liqueur
▶ 2 parts (1 fl oz/30 ml) coconut cream
▶ 8 parts (4 fl oz/120 ml) fresh pineapple juice
▶ 5 strawberries

you will also need
▶ ½ cup (4 fl oz/120 ml) crushed ice

bar tools
▶ Highball glass
▶ Blender

Cost ♇♇
Degree of difficulty ◉

Strawberry Colada

Although there are many different fruits grown in the Caribbean, the strawberry is not among them, and we can only assume that Mother Nature was having an off day with that omission—or maybe she just didn't anticipate the creation of the Piña Colada, which is especially good with a few strawberries added...

preparation In advance: Chill the glass.

mixing Blend the ingredients, reserving one perfect strawberry, until smooth. Serve in the glass.

garnish Garnish with the reserved strawberry.

mixing ingredients
▶ 1 banana, unpeeled
▶ 2 parts (1 fl oz/30 ml) white rum
▶ 2 parts (1 fl oz/30 ml) dark rum
▶ 2 parts (1 fl oz/30 ml) coconut cream
▶ 6 parts (3 fl oz/90 ml) fresh pineapple juice

you will also need
▶ Pineapple wedge
▶ Maraschino cherry
▶ Cocktail umbrella

bar tools
▶ as above

Cost ♇♇
Degree of difficulty ◉

Banana Colada

It's tempting to call this a Banaña Colada! If nothing else, it might distract those who mutter darkly that an authentic colada simply cannot be made with bananas. Well, they have a point—piña colada means "strained pineapple," and it's absolutely impossible to strain the juice out of a banana!

preparation In advance: Chill the glass and freeze the banana, unpeeled, for 1 hour.

mixing Peel and slice the chilled banana and blend the ingredients until smooth. Serve in the glass.

garnish Garnish with a pineapple wedge, a maraschino cherry, and a cocktail umbrella.

Piña Colada

In San Juan, the capital of Puerto Rico, an elegant colonial building housing the restaurant Barrachina bears a plaque: "The house where in 1963 the piña colada was created by Don Ramon Portas Mingot." That's their story and they're sticking to it, although it seems that Don Ramon was responsible not for the creation of this gorgeous cocktail, but for its refinement. Don Ramon, we salute you—nothing conjures up images of sunshine and blue skies quite like a piña colada.

preparation In advance: Chill the glass.

mixing Shake the ingredients briskly with ice. Strain over ice in the glass.

garnish Garnish with a pineapple wedge, a maraschino cherry, and a cocktail umbrella.

Like this?
Try this
▸ **Yum-Yum,**
page 174

mixing ingredients
▸ 2 parts (1 fl oz/30 ml) white rum
▸ 2 parts (1 fl oz/30 ml) coconut cream (or 1½ parts/ ¾ fl oz/22.5 ml coconut cream and ½ part/½ fl oz/ 7.5 ml Malibu®)
▸ 6 parts (3 fl oz/90 ml) fresh pineapple juice

you will also need
▸ Ice cubes
▸ Pineapple wedge
▸ Maraschino cherry
▸ Cocktail umbrella

bar tools
▸ Highball glass
▸ Cocktail shaker
▸ Strainer

Cost ᕰᕰ
Degree of difficulty

Screwdriver

Once you get over the fact that your drink shares its name with a really useful tool (you know, the one you always need and can never find), this is a great cocktail. If you're dying to know why it's called a Screwdriver ... well, some people lose their bar spoons but always have a screwdriver handy to stir their cocktails! The Screwdriver was invented in the early 1950s, using orange juice concentrate. Resist the urge to follow suit—it tastes much better with fresh juice. Just squeeze it straight in...

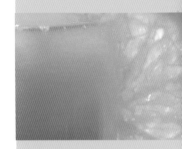

mixing ingredients
▸ 3 parts (1½ fl oz/45 ml) vodka
▸ 1 orange, halved

you will also need
▸ Ice cubes
▸ Half an orange slice

bar tools
▸ Lowball glass
▸ Bar spoon

Cost ￥￥
Degree of difficulty 🍊

preparation In advance: Chill the glass.

mixing Pour the vodka over ice in the glass. Squeeze in the orange juice and stir well.

garnish Garnish with half an orange slice.

Like this? Try this
▸ **Harvey Wallbanger,** *page 118*

Like this? Try this
▸ **Zombie,** *page 182*

Alien Sky

mixing ingredients
▸ 8 parts (4 fl oz/120 ml) fresh pineapple juice
▸ 4 parts (2 fl oz/60 ml) freshly squeezed orange juice
▸ 2 parts (1 fl oz/30 ml) white rum
▸ 2 parts (1 fl oz/30 ml) apricot or cherry brandy
▸ 1½ parts (¾ fl oz/22.5 ml) blue curaçao

you will also need
▸ Ice cubes
▸ Carambola slice

bar tools
▸ Highball glass
▸ Cocktail shaker
▸ Strainer

Cost ¥¥¥
Degree of difficulty

Come on, confess—there's a bit of you that believes there are aliens zooming around in the sky, keeping an eye on what we're up to here on Earth. Imagine the scene at the Monday team meeting: "Listen up, fellow aliens. I saw someone put blocks of frozen water in a container, and then some liquid from different bottles. He put a lid on the container, and shook it very hard. Then he poured out the liquid, drank it, and SMILED. Let *us* try that!" And thus the Alien Sky was created...

preparation In advance: Chill the glass.

mixing Mix the pineapple and orange juice together and pour over ice in the glass. Shake the rum, apricot or cherry brandy, and blue curaçao briskly with ice and strain carefully over the juice.

garnish Garnish with a carambola slice.

Russian Spring

The best thing about spring is that, even though it happens every year, it still seems to come as a surprise when the world comes alive, lovely, fresh, and verdant—exactly like this cocktail, in fact! This recipe—a variation on the original, created by the British cocktail guru Dick Bradsell—epitomizes the season with its gorgeous color and fresh taste of apple and mint. You can use club soda for the fizz, but surely the arrival of another magical spring truly deserves that celebratory splash of champagne ...

preparation In advance: Chill the glass.

mixing Shake all the ingredients, except the champagne, briskly with ice. Strain into the glass and top up with champagne.

garnish Garnish with slices of apple and kiwifruit.

mixing ingredients
▶ 2 parts (1 fl oz/30 ml) vodka
▶ 1 part (½ fl oz/15 ml) green crème de menthe
▶ 2 parts (1 fl oz/30 ml) fresh apple juice
▶ champagne or club soda, to top up

you will also need
▶ Ice cubes
▶ Apple slice
▶ Kiwifruit slice

bar tools
▶ Highball glass
▶ Cocktail shaker
▶ Strainer

Like this? Try this
▶ **Cranberry Champagne Cocktail,** *page 176*

Cost
Degree of difficulty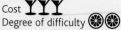

Bloody Mary

mixing ingredients
▸ 3 parts (1½ fl oz/45 ml) vodka
▸ 6 parts (3 fl oz/90 ml) tomato juice
▸ 1 part (½ fl oz/15 ml) freshly squeezed lemon juice
▸ 2 drops Tabasco® sauce
▸ 2 drops Worcestershire® sauce
▸ pinch salt and freshly ground black pepper

you will also need
▸ Ice cubes
▸ Celery stalk
▸ Cocktail umbrella

bar tools
▸ Lowball or stemmed glass
▸ Cocktail shaker
▸ Strainer

Cost ΥΥ
Degree of difficulty

Like this? Try this
▸ **Runner's Mark,** *page 123*

There are many who have reason to be grateful to the late Fernand Petiot, head bartender of New York's St. Regis Hotel from 1934 to 1966, who spiced up the original bland recipe of tomato juice and vodka... Bloody Mary is the quintessential "hair of the dog" cocktail. It might seem insane to drink vodka to cure a hangover, especially if drinking vodka was the cause of the hangover in the first place, but it works— the vodka lifts your gloom, while the tomato juice soothes your irate liver.

preparation In advance: Chill the glass.

mixing Shake the ingredients briskly with ice. Strain over ice in the glass.

garnish Garnish with a celery stalk and a cocktail umbrella.

Danish Mary

Just because you're hungover doesn't mean you can't be adventurous! This version of the "Mary" is made with aquavit (say *akvavit*), which is similar to vodka but has a few things added, typically caraway and coriander seed, anise, dill, and fennel—all extremely good for settling that troubled digestive system.

preparation In advance: Chill the glass.

mixing Shake the ingredients briskly with ice. Strain over ice in the glass.

garnish Garnish with a celery stalk.

mixing ingredients
▸ 4 parts (2 fl oz/60 ml) aquavit
▸ 8 parts (4 fl oz/120 ml) tomato juice
▸ 1 teaspoon freshly squeezed lemon juice
▸ 2 drops each Tabasco® and Worcestershire® sauce
▸ pinch celery salt and freshly ground black pepper

you will also need
▸ Ice cubes
▸ Celery stalk

bar tools
▸ see Bloody Mary, page 150

Cost ▼▼
Degree of difficulty 🌑🌑

Highland Mary

If you think "Highland Mary" sounds rather too genteel for this cocktail, you can use its other name—Bloody Scotsman. Let's face it, this one *is* rather going to sort out the men from the boys! It's also going to set to rights your morning-after symptoms in record time—no hangover will dare to challenge this...

preparation In advance: Chill the glass.

mixing Shake the ingredients briskly with ice. Strain over ice in the glass.

garnish Garnish with the sprig of rosemary, lightly crushed.

mixing ingredients
▸ 2 parts (1 fl oz/30 ml) Scotch whisky
▸ 4 parts (2 fl oz/60 ml) tomato juice
▸ 1 teaspoon shredded onion
▸ 1 teaspoon Worcestershire® sauce
▸ 6 drops Tabasco® sauce
▸ pinch freshly ground black pepper

you will also need
▸ Ice cubes
▸ Fresh rosemary sprig

bar tools
▸ see Bloody Mary, page 150

Cost ▼▼
Degree of difficulty 🌑🌑

French Martini

The American satirist H.L. Mencken described the martini as "the only American invention as perfect as the sonnet." If that's true, then the French Martini—created in the romantic setting of a Loire Valley château south of Paris—is an entire anthology of poetry. The magic ingredient is Chambord®, a raspberry liqueur with hints of blackberry, vanilla, citrus, and honey, and a little kick of cognac. The original recipe dates from the late 17th century, and was much savored by King Louis XIV of France. No wonder he was called "the Sun King"—one sip is enough to make anyone light up!

mixing ingredients
▶ 3 parts (1½ fl oz/45 ml) vodka
▶ 1 part (½ oz/15 ml) Chambord® or raspberry liqueur
▶ 1 part (½ oz/15 ml) fresh pineapple juice

you will also need
▶ Ice cubes
▶ Lime wedge

bar tools
▶ Stemmed cocktail glass
▶ Cocktail shaker
▶ Strainer

Cost ¥¥
Degree of difficulty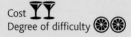

preparation In advance: Chill the glass.

mixing Shake the ingredients briskly with ice. Strain into the glass.

garnish Garnish with a lime wedge.

Like this? Try this
▶ **Raspberry Cosmopolitan,** *page 142*

Like this?
Try this
▸ **Tom Collins,**
page 107

Gin Fizz

mixing ingredients
▸ 4 parts (2 fl oz/60 ml) gin
▸ 1½ parts (¾ fl oz/22.5 ml)
freshly squeezed lemon juice
▸ 1 teaspoon sugar
▸ club soda, to top up

you will also need
▸ Ice cubes
▸ Lemon slice

bar tools
▸ Highball glass
▸ Cocktail shaker
▸ Strainer

Cost 𝖄𝖄
Degree of difficulty

The 1887 edition of the *Bar-tender's Guide* (originally written by Jerry Thomas, "the father of American mixology") includes six recipes for a cocktail with the irresistible word "fizz" in the title—how can you possibly feel anything but great after drinking something called a fizz? The Gin Fizz is the best known and most popular of the breed, but there are some interesting variations: Add an egg white to the shaker and you have a Silver Fizz; add an egg yolk for a Golden Fizz; or avoid the messy business of separating the egg by using the whole thing, and you have a Royal Fizz!

preparation In advance: Chill the glass.

mixing Shake the ingredients, except the soda, briskly with ice. Strain over ice in the glass and top up with soda.

garnish Garnish with a lemon slice.

Chicago Fizz

Chicago, Chigaco, that toddlin' town...
The lyrics of the oft-recorded 1922 song might not
scan perfectly, but the sentiment is wonderful, and if
indeed people were having "the time, the time of their
life" there, it's quite possibly because they quaffed this
scrumptious cocktail! Take it away, ol' blue eyes!

preparation In advance: Chill the glass.

mixing Shake the ingredients, except the soda, briskly with
ice. Strain over ice in the glass and top up with soda.

mixing ingredients
▶ 2 parts (1 fl oz/30 ml)
white rum
▶ 2 parts (1 fl oz/30 ml) port
▶ 2 parts (1 fl oz/30 ml)
freshly squeezed lemon juice
▶ 1 teaspoon sugar
▶ 1 egg white
▶ club soda, to top up

you will also need
▶ Ice cubes

bar tools
▶ Highball glass
▶ Cocktail shaker
▶ Strainer

Cost ♈♈
Degree of difficulty

Sloe Gin Fizz

Gin infused with sugar and sloes, the fruit of
the blackthorn tree, is just delicious. If you've never tried
it, now is the time. Sloe Gin Fizz is another of those
cocktails that seem to inspire lyricists—it turns up in
the most unexpected of songs, and perhaps even more
curiously is the tipple of the bank robbers in the 1998
movie *Safe Men*. And yet it sounds so *sedate*...

preparation In advance: Chill the glass.

mixing Shake the ingredients, except the soda, briskly with
ice. Strain over ice in the glass and top up with soda.

mixing ingredients
▶ 2 parts (1 fl oz/30 ml) gin
▶ 2 parts (1 fl oz/30 ml)
sloe gin
▶ 1½ parts (¾ fl oz/22.5 ml)
freshly squeezed lemon juice
▶ 1 teaspoon sugar
▶ club soda, to top up

you will also need
▶ Ice cubes

bar tools
▶ Highball glass
▶ Cocktail shaker
▶ Strainer

Cost ♈♈
Degree of difficulty

6
Let's party

Like this? Try this
▶ **Blood Orange Bellini,** *page 167*

Buck's Fizz

A Buck's Fizz is a member of the Fizz family—no, not a hyperactive dance troupe, but a cocktail that includes citrus juice and something fizzy. Buck's Fizz, a particularly chic example made with fresh orange juice, champagne, and perhaps just a touch of grenadine, was first served at the Buck's Club in London in 1921. The Mimosa, the slightly later (1925) version claimed by the Paris Ritz, named for the yellow flowers of the mimosa tree, adds Grand Marnier® rather than grenadine. Either way, as you might imagine, the flavor is especially good if you use a quality champagne for this most stylish accompaniment to a sociable weekend brunch.

mixing ingredients
▶ 3 parts (1½ fl oz/45 ml) freshly squeezed orange juice
▶ 6 parts (3 fl oz/90 ml) good-quality champagne
▶ ½ teaspoon grenadine (optional)

you will also need
▶ Orange slice

bar tools
▶ Champagne flute
▶ Cocktail stirrer

Cost ¥¥
Degree of difficulty

preparation In advance: Chill the orange juice, champagne, and the glass.

mixing Pour the orange juice and champagne into the glass and stir once. Add the grenadine if using.

garnish Garnish with an orange slice.

Grass Skirt

Whether you're planning a celebration party or a chasin'-the-blues get together, "Hawaiian" is a great theme. Have your guests come dressed in their most colorful clothes—somber shades are strictly forbidden. Welcome everyone with a lei and give them a generous glass of this delicious cocktail. When your guests are as chilled as their drinks, put on some Hawaiian music and get them all to HULA! You'll soon feel the warmth of that tropical sunshine, whatever the weather!

preparation In advance: Chill the glass.

mixing Shake the ingredients briskly with ice. Strain into the glass over ice and fresh pineapple chunks.

mixing ingredients
▸ 3 parts (1½ fl oz/45 ml) gin
▸ 2 parts (1 fl oz/30 ml) triple sec
▸ 2 parts (1 fl oz/30 ml) fresh pineapple juice
▸ 1 part (½ fl oz/15 ml) grenadine

you will also need
▸ Ice cubes
▸ Fresh pineapple chunks

bar tools
▸ Highball glass
▸ Cocktail shaker
▸ Strainer

Cost ΥΥ
Degree of difficulty

Like this?
Try this
▸ **French Martini,**
page 152

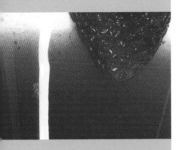

Strawberry Daiquiri

This is a divine cocktail for a summer garden party, and it's so easy—no shaking, no straining, just a quick whiz in the blender. When everything is smooth, have a taste—if the strawberries were a little tart, you might need to add more sugar. Do this if necessary and taste again. Actually, taste it again anyway. Decant it into the chilled pitcher and taste again to check the temperature. Now have another taste—can anything really be that delicious? Better taste a bit more to make sure... Guests? What guests?

SERVES 10

mixing ingredients
▶ 1¼ cups (10 fl oz/300 ml) white rum
▶ ⅔ cup (5 fl oz/150 ml) strawberry schnapps
▶ 1¼ cups (10 fl oz/300 ml) freshly squeezed lime juice
▶ ⅓ –½ cup (about 2 oz/ 60 g) powdered sugar
▶ 10 oz/285 g fresh strawberries

you will also need
▶ Ice cubes
▶ Fresh strawberries

bar tools
▶ Stemmed cocktail glasses
▶ Pitcher
▶ Blender

Cost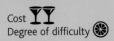
Degree of difficulty ⊛

preparation In advance: Chill the glasses and the pitcher.

mixing Blend all the ingredients until smooth. Pour over ice in the pitcher and serve immediately.

garnish Garnish each glass with a fresh whole strawberry.

Like this? Try this
▶ **Strawberry Mai Tai,** *page 95*

Like this? Try this
▶ **Tropical Martini,** *page 139*

Red Cloud

Red clouds are dramatic. A red sky at night, so they say, indicates "sailor's delight"—fine weather the next day. A red sky in morning is a warning that those same sailors should head for home and do some chores instead. The 19th-century Native American war leader Red Cloud left such an impression that an entire conflict is named in his honor. And a Red Cloud cocktail? Its message is simple—no chores, no wars, just delight!

mixing ingredients
▶ 3 parts (1½ fl oz/45 ml) gin
▶ 1 part (½ fl oz/15 ml) apricot brandy
▶ 1 part (½ fl oz/15 ml) freshly squeezed lemon juice
▶ 1 teaspoon grenadine
▶ 1 dash Angostura® bitters

you will also need
▶ Ice cubes
▶ Maraschino cherry
▶ Lemon rind curl

bar tools
▶ Stemmed cocktail glass
▶ Cocktail shaker
▶ Strainer

Cost
Degree of difficulty

preparation In advance: Chill the glass.

mixing Shake the ingredients briskly with ice. Strain into the glass over ice.

garnish Garnish with a maraschino cherry tucked in a lemon rind curl.

Silver Cloud

There are some people who say that their glass is half full, while others say that it's half empty. Similarly, there are those who believe that every cloud has a silver lining, and others for whom every silver lining has a cloud... Share this delicious cocktail with friends and you'll soon be certain that your glass of Silver Cloud is half full!

preparation In advance: Chill the glass.

mixing Pour the amaretto, coffee liqueur, and milk over ice in the glass and stir well.

garnish Garnish with a spoonful of whipped cream.

mixing ingredients
▶ 2 parts (1 fl oz/30 ml) amaretto
▶ 2 parts (1 fl oz/30 ml) coffee liqueur
▶ 8 parts (4 fl oz/120 ml) whole milk

you will also need
▶ Ice cubes
▶ Whipped cream

bar tools
▶ Highball glass
▶ Bar spoon

Cost ￥￥
Degree of difficulty

White Cloud

There are all sorts of white clouds. Some are wispy, almost transparent, and keep their distance from Earth. Others sit much closer to Earth, join up with their friends, turn gray, and rain down on you. But the best clouds are the fat, fluffy ones that scud along cheerfully in a bright blue sky... The White Cloud cocktail is definitely one of those!

preparation In advance: Chill the glass.

mixing Shake the ingredients briskly over ice. Strain into the glass.

mixing ingredients
▶ 3 parts (1½ fl oz/45 ml) vodka
▶ 1½ parts (¾ fl oz/22.5 ml) white crème de cacao
▶ 4 parts (2 fl oz/60 ml) fresh pineapple juice
▶ 1½ parts (¾ fl oz/22.5 ml) light cream

you will also need
▶ Ice cubes

bar tools
▶ Lowball glass
▶ Cocktail shaker
▶ Strainer

Cost ￥￥
Degree of difficulty

Brandy Zoom

mixing ingredients
- 1 tablespoon honey
- 3 parts (1½ fl oz/45 ml) brandy
- 1½ parts (¾ fl oz/22.5 ml) whipping cream

you will also need
- Ice cubes
- Cake garnishes (colored sugar sprinkles, silver balls, etc.)

bar tools
- Lowball or stemmed glass
- Cocktail shaker
- Strainer

Cost 𝖸𝖸
Degree of difficulty 🍊🍊

This is the perfect drink for a party with the girls—so perfect is it, indeed, that it was included on the founding list of a wonderful Boston organization called Ladies United for the Preservation of Endangered Cocktails (LUPEC), whose motto is: "Dismantling the patriarchy ... one drink at a time!" So go for it, all you girls out there whose souls resonate with LUPEC's heartfelt sentiment—sprinkle your unfashionable Brandy Zooms with sugar and spice and all things nice and celebrate being feminine!

preparation In advance: Dissolve the honey in a little hot water.

mixing Shake the ingredients briskly with ice. Strain into the glass.

garnish Garnish with colored sugar sprinkles, silver balls, etc.

Like this? Try this
▶ **Creamsicle,**
page 86

Rose

In times past, the secret language of flowers was used to convey unspoken messages and the rose, of course, still has quite a lot to say for itself. Pink roses stand for love and youth and beauty; white roses speak of tentative new love; yellow roses carry the desperate air of love unrequited. And red? Well, as everyone knows, the red rose is the symbol of passionate love. The Rose cocktail is very definitely red. Who will you be sharing yours with?

preparation In advance: Chill the glass.

mixing Shake the ingredients briskly with ice. Strain into the glass.

garnish Garnish with a maraschino cherry.

Like this? Try this
▶ **Carambola Cocktail,** *page 138*

mixing ingredients
▶ 3 parts (1½ fl oz/45 ml) dry vermouth
▶ 1 part (½ fl oz/15 ml) kirsch
▶ 2 teaspoons cherry brandy

you will also need
▶ Ice cubes
▶ Maraschino cherry

bar tools
▶ Stemmed cocktail glass
▶ Cocktail shaker
▶ Strainer

Cost ℤℤℤ
Degree of difficulty

Bellini

The Bellini is perfect for a party. It's beautiful to look at, delicate in taste, and there's a charming story behind the name—so if you hit a conversational low point, you can at least discuss your drinks! The story goes like this: The cocktail was invented by Giuseppe Cipriani, who opened Harry's Bar in Venice in 1931. The color reminded him of a painting of a saint by the Venetian Renaissance artist Giovanni Bellini, so he named his new cocktail in Bellini's honor... plenty to talk about there!

mixing ingredients
▶ 2 parts (1 fl oz/30 ml) fresh white peach purée
▶ 6 parts (3 fl oz/90 ml) prosecco

you will also need
▶ Maraschino cherry

bar tools
▶ Champagne flute
▶ Cocktail stirrer

Cost 🍸🍸
Degree of difficulty

preparation In advance: Freeze the white peach purée. Chill the prosecco and the glass.

mixing Pour the frozen white peach purée into the glass, slowly add the prosecco, and stir gently.

garnish Garnish with a maraschino cherry.

Like this? Try this
▶ **Buck's Fizz,** *page 158*

Strawberry Bellini

There are those who declare it sacrilegious to use yellow peaches instead of white for making a Bellini, so it's easy to imagine what they'd say about using strawberries... A Strawberry Bellini is very feminine—so, ladies, it's the ideal cocktail for a bridal shower, a baby shower, or simply for unwinding after your end-of-a-long-day shower.

preparation In advance: Chill the strawberry purée, the prosecco, and the glass.

mixing Pour the chilled strawberry purée into the glass, slowly add the prosecco, and stir gently.

garnish Garnish with a fresh strawberry.

mixing ingredients
▶ 2 parts (1 fl oz/30 ml) sweetened fresh strawberry purée, strained
▶ 6 parts (3 fl oz/90 ml) prosecco

you will also need
▶ Small fresh strawberry

bar tools
▶ Champagne flute
▶ Cocktail stirrer

Cost 🍸🍸
Degree of difficulty ●

Blood Orange Bellini

The Blood Orange Bellini has a very empowering ring to its name—this is the cocktail to order when you need to "gird your loins." Try saying, very softly and meekly, "I'd like a Blood Orange Bellini, please." It's almost impossible! Now say it with the determination it demands, and you'll be ready to take on the world...

preparation In advance: Chill the blood orange juice, the prosecco, and the glass.

mixing Pour the chilled blood orange juice into the glass, slowly add the prosecco, and stir gently.

garnish Garnish with a maraschino cherry.

mixing ingredients
▶ 2 parts (1 fl oz/30 ml) freshly squeezed blood orange juice, unstrained
▶ 8 parts (4 fl oz/120 ml) prosecco

you will also need
▶ Maraschino cherry

bar tools
▶ Champagne flute
▶ Cocktail stirrer

Cost 🍸🍸
Degree of difficulty

mixing ingredients
▶ 2 parts (1 fl oz/30 ml) amaretto
▶ 10 parts (5 fl oz/150 ml) champagne

you will also need
▶ Lemon zest twist

bar tools
▶ Champagne flute

Cost ㄒㄒ
Degree of difficulty 🍊

Kir Imperial

The Kir Imperial is often made with raspberry liqueur, but this version uses the Italian liqueur amaretto, so it's a little different—nutty, not fruity. The word "amaretto" sounds *so* romantic... however, it is derived not from *amore*, the Italian word for love, but from *amaro*, which means "bitter" and refers to nothing more than the flavor of the almonds used to make this liqueur.

---

preparation In advance: Chill the champagne and the glass.

mixing Pour the amaretto into the glass and top up with the champagne.

garnish Garnish with a lemon zest twist.

---

mixing ingredients
▶ 1 part (½ fl oz/15 ml) crème de cassis
▶ 1 dash Calvados
▶ Normandy cider, to top up

bar tools
▶ Champagne flute

Cost ㄒㄒㄒ
Degree of difficulty 🍊

Kir Normand

The good news about the Kir Normand is that cider is less demanding on the budget than champagne. The bad news is that Calvados is quite expensive—but you only need a dash and you can buy it in miniature bottles. If you can't find genuine Normandy cider, look for a good-quality dry, sparkling, hard apple cider and teach it to speak French (the last bit isn't essential).

---

preparation In advance: Chill the cider and the glass.

mixing Pour the crème de cassis into the glass, add a dash of Calvados, and top up with the cider.

Like this? Try this
▶ **Strawberry Bellini,** *page 167*

Kir Royal

Kir is named for an enterprising mayor of Dijon, in the French province of Burgundy—not only did Félix Kir pioneer town twinning ("sister cities") after World War II, he also got everyone hooked on the aperitif of local white Aligoté wine and crème de cassis (black currant liqueur) that he served at town hall receptions. *Blanc-cass*, as it was known, had already been around for a hundred years, but after Mayor Kir's sterling efforts it could bear no other name but his. Kir Royal, one of several variations, is made—as you might guess—with champagne.

preparation In advance: Chill the champagne and the glass.

mixing Pour the crème de cassis into the glass and top up with the champagne (one part crème de cassis to ten parts champagne).

Garnish Garnish with a maraschino cherry.

SERVES 10
mixing ingredients
▶ ⅔ cup (5 fl oz/150 ml) crème de cassis
▶ 2 bottles (2 x 750 ml) champagne

you will also need
▶ Maraschino cherry

bar tools
▶ Champagne flute

Cost ▼▼
Degree of difficulty ◉

Kamikaze

The Kamikaze shooter isn't quite as lethal as the World War II suicide attacks by Japanese kamikaze pilots, for whom a sudden and horrible demise was inevitable, but it's still wise to take a few simple precautions before imbibing, especially if you're going to do the job properly and knock your cocktail back in one. First, ask a responsible person to hide your car keys until the following day, at least. Now make sure there's no one around who you want to impress—you might soon be in a state where the impression you leave is rather less than impressive! Finally, check your surroundings. Is there a big, soft couch nearby, onto which you can collapse without causing yourself injury? Excellent! You're good to go...

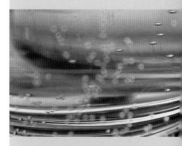

mixing ingredients
▸ 2 parts (1 fl oz/30 ml) vodka
▸ 2 parts (1 fl oz/30 ml) blue curaçao
▸ 2 parts (1 fl oz/30 ml) freshly squeezed lime juice

you will also need
▸ Ice cubes

bar tools
▸ Double shot glass
▸ Mixing glass
▸ Bar spoon
▸ Strainer

Cost ΥΥ
Degree of difficulty ✹

preparation In advance: Chill the shot glass and the mixing glass.

mixing Stir the ingredients with ice in the mixing glass. Strain into the shot glass.

Like this? Try this
▸ **Blue Lagoon,** *page 97*

Cosmopolitan

mixing ingredients
▸ 3 parts (1½ fl oz/45 ml) lemon vodka
▸ 1 part (½ fl oz/15 ml) cranberry juice
▸ 2 teaspoons orange liqueur
▸ 2 lime wedges (to produce 2 teaspoons juice)

you will also need
▸ Ice cubes

bar tools
▸ Stemmed cocktail glass
▸ Cocktail shaker
▸ Strainer

Cost ΥΥ
Degree of difficulty 🍊🍊

If you're a fan of the TV comedy-drama *Sex and the City*, you'll be familiar with one of the show's greatest icons, the Cosmopolitan cocktail ("Cosmo," as it is fondly known). It's the favorite drink of Carrie Bradshaw, who on one occasion even asks for a Cosmopolitan to accompany her cheeseburger and fries from a drive-through. So when you're spending a weekend with your friends watching the boxed set of the whole six seasons, followed by the movie, what other cocktail can you possibly drink?

preparation In advance: Chill the glass. Just before preparing the cocktail, squeeze the juice from the lime wedges into the shaker and drop in the wedges.

mixing Shake the ingredients briskly with ice. Strain into the glass.

Like this? Try this
▸ **Ink Martini,** *page 36*

Blue Cosmopolitan

With all the highs and lows experienced by the *Sex and the City* girls as they journeyed through life on their emotional rollercoaster, they could have used the Cosmo as a mood indicator when they met, ordering the original pink Cosmo when things were looking rosy, and this Blue Cosmo when life wasn't going so well...

preparation In advance: Chill the glass.

mixing Shake the ingredients briskly with ice. Strain into the glass.

garnish Garnish with a lemon zest twist.

mixing ingredients
▶ 4 parts (2 fl oz/60 ml) lemon vodka
▶ 1 part (½ fl oz/15 ml) blue curaçao
▶ 3 parts (1½ oz/45 ml) white cranberry juice
▶ 1 teaspoon freshly squeezed lime juice

you will also need
▶ Ice cubes
▶ Lemon zest twist

bar tools
▶ Stemmed cocktail glass
▶ Cocktail shaker
▶ Strainer

Cost **ΥΥ**
Degree of difficulty

White Cosmopolitan

White cranberry juice is perfect for making Cosmos in any color other than the original pink. But hold on—aren't cranberries red? Yes, cranberries are indeed red—when they're completely ripe. Before that, they're white and have a sweeter, more delicate flavor that works really well in this pale and interesting cocktail.

preparation In advance: Chill the glass.

mixing Shake the ingredients briskly with ice. Strain into the glass.

garnish Garnish with half a lime slice.

mixing ingredients
▶ 3 parts (1½ fl oz/45 ml) vodka
▶ 1 part (½ fl oz/15 ml) orange liqueur
▶ 2 parts (1 oz/30 ml) white cranberry juice
▶ 2 teaspoons freshly squeezed lemon juice

you will also need
▶ Ice cubes
▶ Half a lime slice

bar tools
▶ Stemmed cocktail glass
▶ Cocktail shaker
▶ Strainer

Cost **ΥΥ**
Degree of difficulty

Like this? Try this
▸ **Piña Colada,** *page 145*

Yum-Yum

mixing ingredients
▸ 3 parts (1½ fl oz/45 ml) white rum
▸ 1 part (1½ fl oz/15 ml) coconut rum
▸ 2 parts (1 fl oz/30 ml) fresh mango juice
▸ 2 parts (1 fl oz/30 ml) fresh peach juice
▸ 1 teaspoon peach liqueur
▸ 2 teaspoons freshly squeezed lime juice

you will also need
▸ Ice cubes
▸ Lime slice twist
▸ Decorative cocktail pick

bar tools
▸ Stemmed cocktail glass
▸ Cocktail shaker
▸ Strainer

Cost ΥΥ
Degree of difficulty

According to the dictionary, yum-yum is an exclamation "used to express pleasure at eating delicious food"—or, in this case, drinking a delicious cocktail! Yum-Yum has a very childish ring to it—it's the sort of thing you say to a toddler when you're trying to convince him/her that Brussels sprouts are really delicious—and yet it's so expressive that there are occasions when no other word will do. Take your first sip of this cocktail and you'll immediately understand that this is one of those times ...

preparation In advance: Chill the glass.

mixing Shake the ingredients briskly with ice. Strain into the glass.

garnish Garnish with a lime slice twist on a decorative cocktail pick.

Mediterranean Martini

This variation on the classic dry martini is "shaken, not stirred." Only this method will produce a slight frost and create the wonderful, fresh, pale blue of a rain-washed, early morning Mediterranean sky. Drizzle the grenadine into the side of the glass where it will sink gracefully to the bottom of the glass to become the rising sun. It's remarkable how evocative a cocktail can be.... Serve this at a party with some really colorful Mediterranean-style food and a good time will be had by all!

mixing ingredients
▶ 3½ parts (1¾ fl oz/ 52.5 ml) gin
▶ 1 part (½ fl oz/15 ml) dry vermouth
▶ ¼ teaspoon blue curaçao
▶ 1 teaspoon grenadine

you will also need
▶ Ice cubes

bar tools
▶ Stemmed cocktail glass
▶ Cocktail shaker
▶ Strainer

Cost ￥￥￥
Degree of difficulty

preparation In advance: Chill the glass.

mixing Shake the ingredients, except the grenadine, briskly with ice. Strain into the glass and drizzle in the grenadine.

Like this? Try this
▶ **Betty Mac,** *page 39*

Cranberry Champagne Cocktail

SERVES 10

mixing ingredients

▸ ¼ cup (2 fl oz/60 ml) triple sec
▸ 1¼ cups (10 fl oz/300 ml) cranberry juice cocktail
▸ ½ cup (4 fl oz/120 ml) fresh lime juice
▸ 2 tablespoons superfine or granulated sugar
▸ 4 cups (2 pints/1 liter) champagne

you will also need

▸ Ice cubes

bar tools

▸ Pitcher
▸ Champagne flutes
▸ Festive swizzle sticks

Cost ♈♈
Degree of difficulty ◉

Champagne is, of course, the quintessential celebration drink, and nothing will get your guests into party mood faster than an elegant champagne cocktail. The Classic Champagne Cocktail is said to be the inspiration of the winner of a New York cocktail competition in 1899, and consists of a sugar cube soaked in bitters and placed in a champagne flute, covered with brandy, and topped up with champagne. The version here is the perfect cocktail for Thanksgiving and Christmas celebrations, with its glorious cranberry color and hint of orange flavor.

preparation In advance: Stir together the triple sec, cranberry juice, lime juice, and sugar in a pitcher, then cover and chill in the refrigerator for 4 hours. Chill the champagne and the glasses.

mixing Just before serving, add ice cubes to the pitcher, pour in the champagne, and stir to combine. Serve immediately.

Like this? Try this
▸ **Kir Imperial,** *page 168*

The Kiss

The Kiss ... A radiant painting by Gustav Klimt (1862–1918) in a Vienna art gallery; a marble sculpture by Auguste Rodin (1840–1917) in a Paris museum; an irresistible strawberry-flavor cocktail by [insert your own details here, omitting anything you'd sooner not share, such as your year of birth]. It's obvious why the works by Klimt and Rodin bear the name, but the cocktail? Actually, that's obvious too. It's as sweet as a first embrace—just watch out for the vodka kick!

mixing ingredients
▶ 5 parts (2½ fl oz/75 ml) vodka
▶ 3 parts (1½ fl oz/45 ml) strawberry liqueur

you will also need
▶ Ice cubes

bar tools
▶ Lowball glass
▶ Cocktail shaker
▶ Strainer

Cost ⍦⍦
Degree of difficulty

preparation In advance: Chill the glass.

mixing Shake the ingredients briskly with ice. Strain into the glass.

Like this? Try this
▶ **Strawberry Colada,** *page 144*

Like this? Try this
▶ **Mai Tai,**
page 94

Pink Elephant

Pink elephants have long been associated with insobriety, and as a stern reminder of the potential effects of alcoholic excesses we need look no further than Dumbo, Disney's animated pachyderm with the oversized ears that caused him so much trouble, who witnessed a whole parade of imaginary pink elephants after sipping water from a bucket spiked with champagne ... dear reader, he woke up in a tree. Let Dumbo's misfortune be a lesson to *you* ...

mixing ingredients
▶ 1½ parts (¾ fl oz/ 22.5 ml) vodka
▶ 1½ parts (¾ fl oz/ 22.5 ml) vanilla liqueur
▶ 1½ parts (¾ fl oz/ 22.5 ml) crème de noyaux
▶ 1½ parts (¾ fl oz/ 22.5 ml) freshly squeezed orange juice
▶ 1½ parts (¾ fl oz/ 22.5 ml) light cream
▶ grenadine, to taste

you will also need
▶ Ice cubes
▶ Pineapple leaf
▶ Lime wedge
▶ Orange segment
▶ Maraschino cherry

bar tools
▶ Highball glass
▶ Bar spoon

Cost ♈♈♈
Degree of difficulty ✻

preparation In advance: Chill the glass.

mixing Stir the ingredients, except the grenadine, briskly with ice. Stir in grenadine to achieve the desired pinkness.

garnish Garnish with a pineapple leaf, a lime wedge, an orange segment, and a maraschino cherry.

Like this? Try this
▸ **White Cosmopolitan,** *page 173*

Flirtini

The Flirtini is an essential cocktail to serve at a party—after all, what are parties for if not to engage in a little flirtation? Incidentally, if you're one of those people with a compelling urge to matchmake, you might take this opportunity to hone your skills in that direction—imagine what a great wedding anecdote it would make if you could claim to have introduced the blushing bride to her adoring groom over a champagne cocktail with the most appropriate name ever!

SERVES 10
mixing ingredients
▸ 2 slices of fresh pineapple, roughly chopped
▸ ⅔ cup (5 fl oz/150 ml) triple sec
▸ ⅔ cup (5 fl oz/150 ml) vodka
▸ 1¼ cups (10 fl oz/300 ml) fresh pineapple juice
▸ 1 x 750 ml bottle of champagne

you will also need
▸ Pineapple wedges

bar tools
▸ Stemmed cocktail glasses
▸ 2 pitchers
▸ Muddler
▸ Bar spoon
▸ Strainer

Cost ΥΥΥ
Degree of difficulty

preparation In advance: Chill the glasses, the pitchers, and the champagne.

mixing Muddle the chopped pineapple with the triple sec in one of the pitchers. Stir in the vodka and the pineapple juice. Just before serving, strain into the second pitcher and add the champagne. Serve in the chilled glasses.

garnish Garnish each glass with a pineapple wedge.

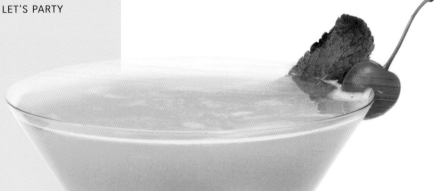

Zombie

mixing ingredients
▶ 1 part (½ fl oz/15 ml) dark rum
▶ 1 part (½ fl oz/15 ml) white rum
▶ 1 part (½ fl oz/15 ml) apricot brandy
▶ 1 part (½ fl oz/15 ml) pineapple juice
▶ ½ teaspoon freshly squeezed orange juice
▶ ½ teaspoon freshly squeezed lemon juice

you will also need
▶ Ice cubes
▶ Cracked ice
▶ Maraschino cherry
▶ Fresh mint sprig

bar tools
▶ Stemmed cocktail glass
▶ Cocktail shaker
▶ Strainer

Cost ¥¥¥
Degree of difficulty

The word "zombie" refers either to a corpse brought back to life by witchcraft, or to a person in a state of complete apathy and mindlessness—there's probably not much to choose between them! The Zombie cocktail is therefore an extremely versatile drink—it can reduce you to that apathetic condition, then revive you again. To achieve this, of course, you'd have to drink it in multiples of two, which is definitely unwise—and this is one of the more benign versions of that powerful cocktail!

preparation In advance: Chill the glass.

mixing Shake the ingredients briskly with ice. Strain over cracked ice in the glass.

garnish Garnish with a maraschino cherry and a fresh mint sprig.

Like this? Try this
▶ **Red Cloud,** page 162

Electric Lemonade

Lemonade is a drink that frequently pops up in traditional children's literature. It gets a starring role in virtually everything written by the British author Enid Blyton. *The Anne of Green Gables Cookbook* includes a recipe for the old-fashioned lemonade enjoyed by the irrepressible Anne and her friends. Lemonade stands manned by enterprising children are undisputed icons of the American summer. Lemonade is wholesome, unsophisticated, and innocent. But Electric Lemonade? Now, that's a completely different story...

preparation In advance: Chill the glass.

mixing Pour the vodka, blue curaçao, and sweet and sour mix over ice in the glass. Top up with lemon-lime soda.

garnish Garnish with a lime slice.

mixing ingredients
▶ 3 parts (1½ fl oz/45 ml) lemon vodka
▶ 1 part (½ fl oz/15 ml) blue curaçao
▶ 4 parts (2 fl oz/60 ml) sweet and sour mix
▶ lemon-lime soda, to top up

you will also need
▶ Ice cubes
▶ Lime slice

bar tools
▶ Highball glass

Cost **ΥΥ**
Degree of difficulty ✹

Like this? Try this
▶ **Blue Cosmopolitan,** *page 173*

Fireworks

Two things are essential to a celebration with attitude—champagne and fireworks. But while the champagne is manageable for a private party, fireworks are something of a hassle to organize. So here's an excellent compromise—champagne AND fireworks in a glass! Serve this vibrant cocktail as your guests arrive to start the party with a bang, or save it for the end of the event and serve it in lieu of the loud, slightly scary, real thing ...

mixing ingredients
▸ 3 parts (1½ fl oz/45 ml) tangerine schnapps
▸ 2 parts (1 fl oz/30 ml) gin
▸ 1 part (½ fl oz/15 ml) freshly squeezed tangerine juice, unstrained
▸ champagne, to top up

you will also need
▸ Granulated sugar
▸ Tangerine segment
▸ Ice cubes

bar tools
▸ Stemmed cocktail glass
▸ Cocktail shaker
▸ Strainer

Cost ᵧᵧᵧ
Degree of difficulty ✹✹

preparation In advance: Chill the glass. Just before serving, scatter some sugar on a paper towel. Rub the tangerine segment around the rim of the glass, then dip the rim into the sugar.

mixing Shake the ingredients, except the champagne, briskly with ice. Strain into the glass and top up with champagne.

Like this? Try this
▸ **Betty Blue,** *page 38*

Fire Starter

"Fire Starter" is putting it mildly—this cocktail is only one step away from pyromania! You might well look at the ingredients and wonder if there's anything that *doesn't* go into it, and it's true that there's a fruitbowl of flavors in there—but if you're going to start a fire, you need plenty of fuel...

preparation In advance: Chill the glass.

mixing Pour all the ingredients over ice in the glass and stir well.

mixing ingredients
▸ 3 parts (1½ fl oz/45 ml) vodka
▸ 2 parts (1 fl oz/30 ml) orange liqueur
▸ 2 parts (1 fl oz/30 ml) peach schnapps
▸ 2 parts (1 fl oz/30 ml) sloe gin
▸ 3 parts (1½ fl oz/45 ml) cola

you will also need
▸ Ice cubes

bar tools
▸ Highball glass
▸ Bar spoon

Cost ♈♈♈
Degree of difficulty 🍊

Fireman's Sour

Where there's a fire, there must be a Fireman. Firefighters are possibly THE most admired of men, although in some cases, let's face it, it's debatable whether it's their heroic deeds or their uniform that makes the heart flutter... Either way, a cool cocktail will help to quell any stray flames of ardor!

preparation In advance: Chill the glass.

mixing Shake the ingredients, except the club soda, briskly with ice. Strain into the glass and top up with club soda.

mixing ingredients
▸ 4 parts (2 fl oz/60 ml) white rum
▸ 4 parts (2 fl oz/60 ml) freshly squeezed lime juice
▸ 1 part (½ fl oz/15 ml) grenadine
▸ 2 parts (1 fl oz/30 ml) club soda

you will also need
▸ Ice cubes
▸ Lemon zest twist

bar tools
▸ Highball glass
▸ Cocktail shaker
▸ Strainer

Cost ♈♈
Degree of difficulty

Eggnog

This is one cocktail where no ice is required—unless you're going to drink it after ice-skating, of course! Traditionally served around the Christmas holiday season, it's likely that eggnog originated in England and arrived in the North American colonies during the 18th century. It's probably a version of posset, a medieval concoction of hot, spiced milk curdled with wine or ale and sipped as a remedy for minor ailments, although these days it's more usually served at room temperature or chilled. Now, where are those ice-skates?…

preparation In advance: Place the egg yolks, sugar, and vanilla extract in a large bowl and beat with an electric hand-mixer for 10 minutes, or until firm. Gradually add the rum and brandy. Chill in the refrigerator until required. You can do this bit a few hours in advance. Just before serving, stir in the milk and nutmeg. Beat the cream and the egg whites until stiff, in separate bowls.

mixing Fold the beaten egg whites into the egg yolk mixture, then fold in the cream. Divide among the glass mugs.

garnish Garnish with a little whipped cream, freshly ground nutmeg, and cinnamon sticks.

SERVES 12
mixing ingredients
▶ 12 eggs, separated
▶ 1½ cups (12 oz/350 g) superfine sugar
▶ 1 teaspoon vanilla extract
▶ 2 cups (1 pint/500 ml) dark rum
▶ ¾ cup (6 fl oz/175 ml) brandy
▶ 6 cups (3 pints/1.5 liters) whole milk
▶ 1½ teaspoons freshly ground nutmeg
▶ 2 cups (1 pint/500 ml) heavy cream

you will also need
▶ 2 cups (1 pint/500 ml) heavy cream, lightly whipped
▶ Freshly ground nutmeg
▶ Cinnamon sticks

bar tools
▶ Large bowl
▶ Electric hand-mixer
▶ Glass mugs with handles

Cost **ΥΥΥ**
Degree of difficulty 🍊🍊

PLEASE NOTE that this recipe contains raw eggs and should be avoided by anyone with compromised health.

Like this? Try this
▶ **Brandy Zoom,** *page 164*

Recipe index

General index